75 More Movies to Get Teenagers Talking

Videos That Teach 4

DOUG FIELDS & EDDIE JAMES

ZONDERVAN™

GRAND RAPIDS, MICHIGAN 49530 USA

ZONDERVAN.COM/
AUTHORTRACKER

Youth Specialties
www.youthspecialties.com

Youth Specialties

Videos That Teach 4: 75 More Movie Moments to Get Teenagers Talking
Copyright © 2005 by Doug Fields and Eddie James

Youth Specialties products, 300 South Pierce Street, El Cajon, CA 92020, are published by
Zondervan, 5300 Patterson Avenue SE, Grand Rapids, MI 49530

Library of Congress Cataloging-in-Publication Data
Fields, Doug, 1962-
  Videos that teach 4 : 75 more movie moments to get teenagers talking / Doug Fields
and Eddie James.
    p. cm.
  ISBN-10: 0-310-25662-3 (pbk.)
  ISBN-13: 978-0-310-25662-5 (pbk.)
  1. Motion pictures in Christian education. 2. Christian education of teenagers. I. Title:
Videos that teach four. II. James, Eddie, 1970- III. Title.

BV1535.4.F56 2005
268'.67--dc22

2005024911

Unless otherwise indicated, all Scripture quotations are taken from the *Holy Bible: New
International Version* (North American Edition). Copyright © 1973, 1978, 1984 by
International Bible Society. Used by permission of Zondervan.

Some of the anecdotal illustrations in this book are true to life and are included with
the permission of the persons involved. All other illustrations are composites of real
situations, and any resemblance to people living or dead is coincidental.

Web site addresses listed in this book were current at the time of publication. Please
contact Youth Specialties via e-mail (YS@YouthSpecialties.com) to report URLs that are
no longer operational and replacement URLs if available.

Creative team: Dave Urbanski, Laura Gross, Janie Wilkerson, and Heather Haggerty
Cover and interior design by David Conn
Printed in the United States of America

05 06 07 08 09 10 • 10 9 8 7 6 5 4 3 2 1

Acknowledgments

While we'd like to thank all the people we drag to the movies with us...that's a little unrealistic—even in our fourth book. So we'll break our thanks into big-time thanks and thanks a lot!

Big Time Thanks!
Erin Macdonald and Charissa Fishbeck

Thanks a Lot!
Stephanie James, Tommy Woodard, Merritt Johnston, Ted Lowe, Brian Cropp, Mark Matlock, Tim Sherman, Dennis Beckner, Max and Mark McGill, Monty Fields, Delia Baltierra, Lori Warren, and the Fields children (Torie, Cody, and Cassie) who always love to watch movies.

—*Doug and Eddie*

Contents

Quick Clip Locator—by topic 7
Quick Clip Locator—by Bible reference. 13
A Note from Doug—*Be careful!...A DVD idea...What's different about this book?*. 19
How to Use This Book—*Esther, Everyman, and Ever After...Why use movie clips in youth meetings, anyway?...FAQs...Illustrating or building a lesson with Videos That Teach 4...What you'll find with each clip* 21

The movies (in alphabetical order—**bold clips** are special holiday titles)

13 Going on 30   26
50 First Dates   28
About Schmidt   30
Antwone Fisher (Thanksgiving)   32
**The Best of Saturday Night Live:
Steve Martin** (Independence Day)   34
Big Fish   36
Bobby Jones: Stroke of Genius   38
Bowling for Columbine   40
Bruce Almighty   42
Cast Away   44
A Charlie Brown Christmas
(Christmas)   46
Cheaper by the Dozen (Father's Day)   48
A Christmas Story (1st clip)
(Christmas)   50
A Christmas Story (2nd clip)
(Christmas)   52
Christmas Vacation (Christmas)   54
A Cinderella Story   56
Confessions of a Teenage Drama Queen   58
The Day After Tomorrow   60
Elf (Father's Day)   62
Envy   64
The Family Man (1st clip)
(Valentine's Day)   66
The Family Man (2nd clip)   68
Finding Nemo (Father's Day)   70
Flight of the Phoenix   72
Freaky Friday (Mother's Day)   74
Friday Night Lights   76
Hidalgo   78
Home for the Holidays
(Thanksgiving)   80
The Hours   82

How the Grinch Stole Christmas
(Christmas)   84
I, Robot   86
The Incredibles   88
Jingle All the Way (Christmas)   90
The Joy Luck Club (Mother's Day)   92
King Arthur   94
Life as a House   96
The Lord of the Rings: The Two Towers
(1st clip)   98
The Lord of the Rings: The Two Towers
(2nd clip)   100
The Lord of the Rings: The Two Towers
(3rd clip)   102
Lost in Translation   104
Luther   106
The Matrix Reloaded   108
Mean Girls   110
Miracle (Independence Day)   112
My Big Fat Greek Wedding   114
My Life (1st clip)   116
My Life (2nd clip)   118
My Life (3rd clip)   120
Mystery Men (Halloween)   122
Napoleon Dynamite   124
Notting Hill (Valentine's Day)   126
The Passion of the Christ (1st clip)
(Good Friday and Easter)   128
The Passion of the Christ (2nd clip)
(Good Friday and Easter)   130
The Passion of the Christ (3rd clip)
(Good Friday and Easter)   132
Pay It Forward   134
Pieces of April (Thanksgiving)   136
Planes, Trains, and Automobiles
(Thanksgiving)   138

Radio   140
Raising Helen   142
The Santa Clause (Christmas)   144
Saved!   146
Saving Private Ryan (Memorial Day)   148
Say Anything (Graduation)   150
School of Rock   152
Scrooged (Christmas)   154
Seabiscuit   156
Shrek 2   158
Spider-Man 2   160
The Stepford Wives   162
The Sure Thing   164
The Terminal   166
The Village   168
Win a Date with Tad Hamilton! (1st clip) (Valentine's Day)   170
Win a Date with Tad Hamilton! (2nd clip) (Valentine's Day)   172
Zoolander   174

Quick Clip Locator

BY TOPIC

9-11 Bowling for Columbine *40*
Abandonment Cast Away *44*
Abilities School of Rock *152*
Acceptance Big Fish *36*
Accountability The Lord of the Rings: The Two Towers (2nd clip) *100*
Accusations The Lord of the Rings: The Two Towers (3rd clip) *102*, The Passion of the Christ (2nd clip) *130*
Action Pay It Forward *134*
Affection Win a Date with Tad Hamilton! (1st clip) *170*
Anger Freaky Friday *74*, How the Grinch Stole Christmas *84*, Luther *106*
Anticipation A Christmas Story (2nd clip) *52*
Appearance The Santa Clause *144*, Shrek 2 *158*
Attitude 13 Going on 30 *26*
Attraction Notting Hill *126*
Authority Finding Nemo *70*
Bad habits Hidalgo *78*
Baptism My Big Fat Greek Wedding *114*
Beauty The Santa Clause *144*, Shrek 2 *158*
Being real Big Fish *36*
Being thankful Planes, Trains, and Automobiles *138*
Being yourself A Cinderella Story *56*
Bible I, Robot *86*; The Lord of the Rings: The Two Towers (1st clip) *98*, Lost in Translation *104*, Saved! *146*
Birth of Christ A Charlie Brown Christmas *46*
Bitterness Envy *64*, How the Grinch Stole Christmas *84*, Luther *106*
Blame The Joy Luck Club *92*
Boasting The Joy Luck Club *92*
Calling Zoolander *174*
Chances The Matrix Reloaded *108*

Change My Big Fat Greek Wedding *114*, The Santa Clause *144*
Change the world around you Pay It Forward *134*
Character 13 Going on 30 *26*, Big Fish *36*, Bobby Jones: Stroke of Genius *38*, King Arthur *94*, My Life (3rd clip) *120*, The Santa Clause *144*, Scrooged *154*, Shrek 2 *158*
Charity Scrooged *154*
Childhood 13 Going on 30 *26*
Childhood memories Christmas Vacation *54*, How the Grinch Stole Christmas *84*
Childlike faith My Life (2nd clip) *118*
Choices Cheaper by the Dozen *48*, The Family Man (1st clip) *66*, Hidalgo *78*, The Sure Thing *164*
Christmas traditions Christmas Vacation *54*
Cliques Mean Girls *110*
Coincidence The Matrix Reloaded *108*
Communication Big Fish *36*, The Incredibles *88*, Lost in Translation *104*, Pieces of April *136*
Comparison Envy *64*
Compassion About Schmidt *30*, Napoleon Dynamite *124*
Condemnation The Passion of the Christ (3rd clip) *132*, Saved! *146*, The Village *168*
Confession Confessions of a Teenage Drama Queen *58*
Confusion Luther *106*
Consequences Hidalgo *78*
Consequences of sin The Hours *82*
Conversation A Christmas Story (1st clip) *50*, The Incredibles *88*
Courage King Arthur *94*, Miracle *112*, Napoleon Dynamite *124*, The Passion of the Christ (1st clip) *128*, Spider-Man 2 *160*, The Village *168*
Coveting Envy *64*
Dads Elf *62*

7

Dating The Sure Thing *164*, Win a Date with Tad Hamilton! (1st clip) *170*, Win a Date with Tad Hamilton! (2nd clip) *172*

Death The Day After Tomorrow *60*, Life as a House *96*, My Life (1st clip) *116*, Raising Helen *142*

Decisions The Family Man (2nd clip) *68*

Denial The Passion of the Christ (2nd clip) *130*, The Santa Clause *144*

Desires A Christmas Story (2nd clip) *52*, Envy *64*

Destiny The Family Man (2nd clip) *68*, Flight of the Phoenix *72*

Determination Flight of the Phoenix *72*, The Terminal *166*

Differences Home for the Holidays *80*, Pieces of April *136*

Dignity Bobby Jones: Stroke of Genius *38*

Direction The Matrix Reloaded *108*

Disabilities Radio *140*

Disaster The Day After Tomorrow *60*

Discord Finding Nemo *70*

Disappointment My Life (2nd clip) *118*

Distractions The Lord of the Rings: The Two Towers (3rd clip) *102*

Dominance The Stepford Wives *162*

Double-mindedness The Lord of the Rings: The Two Towers (3rd clip) *102*

Doubt Luther *106*, The Passion of the Christ (1st clip) *128*, Zoolander *174*

Dreams Cheaper by the Dozen *48*, A Christmas Story (1st clip) *50*, School of Rock *152*

Driven The Family Man (2nd clip) *68*

Dynamics The Incredibles *88*

Emotions Confessions of a Teenage Drama Queen *58*, Win a Date with Tad Hamilton! (2nd clip) *172*

End times The Day After Tomorrow *60*

Endurance Miracle *112*

Envy Envy *64*

Equally yoked The Stepford Wives *162*

Eternity Cast Away *44*

Expectations A Christmas Story (1st clip) *50*, Elf *62*, The Family Man (2nd clip) *68*, My Life (2nd clip) *118*, Say Anything *150*

Experience My Life (1st clip) *116*, School of Rock *152*

Failure About Schmidt *30*

False Appearances The Santa Clause *144*

Faith Pay It Forward *134*, The Village *168*

Family 13 Going on 30 *26*, Antwone Fisher *32*, Christmas Vacation *54*, A Cinderella Story *56*, The Family Man (1st clip) *66*, The Family Man (2nd clip) *68*, The Incredibles *88*, My Big Fat Greek Wedding *114*, My Life (1st clip) *116*, Planes, Trains, and Automobiles *138*, Raising Helen *142*

Family relationships Elf *62*, Freaky Friday *74*, The Joy Luck Club *92*, Pieces of April *136*

Fate versus free will The Matrix Reloaded *108*

Father-son bonds My Life (1st clip) *116*

Fear Bowling for Columbine *40*, Life as a House *96*, Napoleon Dynamite *124*, Notting Hill *126*, The Passion of the Christ (2nd clip) *130*, Say Anything *150*, The Village *168*

Fitting in A Cinderella Story *56*, Confessions of a Teenage Drama Queen *58*

Forgiveness 50 First Dates *28*, The Hours *82*

Freedom Finding Nemo *70*, Miracle *112*, Saving Private Ryan *148*

Freedom in Christ The Village *168*

Friendship Friday Night Lights *76*, The Lord of the Rings: The Two Towers (2nd clip) *100*, My Life (3rd clip) *120*, Napoleon Dynamite *124*, Planes, Trains, and Automobiles *138*, Radio *140*, Saved! *146*

Frustration Lost in Translation *104*

Fulfillment Seabiscuit *156*

Future The Family Man (1st clip) *66*, The Family Man (2nd clip) *68*, Say Anything *150*, Scrooged *154*

Generosity Pay It Forward *134*

Gifts Bruce Almighty *42*, A Christmas Story (2nd clip) *52*, Mystery Men *122*, The Santa Clause *144*, School of Rock *152*, Seabiscuit *156*

Giving A Charlie Brown Christmas *46*

Goals Flight of the Phoenix *72*

God The Matrix Reloaded *108*

God's will Lost in Translation *104*, The Passion of the Christ (1st clip) *128*

Going home Home for the Holidays *80*

Good versus evil The Lord of the Rings: The Two Towers (1st clip) *98*

Grace 50 First Dates *28*, Cast Away *44*

Gratitude A Cinderella Story *56*

Greed The Lord of the Rings: The Two Towers (3rd clip) *102*

Grief Raising Helen *142*

Growing up 13 Going on 30 *26*

Guarding emotions Freaky Friday *74*

Guilt 50 First Dates *28*, The Passion of the Christ (3rd clip) *132*

Hate How the Grinch Stole Christmas *84*

Healing The Lord of the Rings: The Two Towers (1st clip) *98*

Hearing God Lost in Translation *104*

Heart Friday Night Lights *76*, The Lord of the Rings: The Two Towers (1st clip) *98*

Heaven The Passion of the Christ (3rd clip) *132*, School of Rock *152*

Heavenly father Elf *62*, The Terminal *166*

Heritage My Life (1st clip) *116*

Heroes Mystery Men *122*

High school Mean Girls *110*

History The Best of Saturday Night Live: Steve Martin *34*

Holiness Saved! *146*

Home Planes, Trains, and Automobiles *138*

Homelessness Planes, Trains, and Automobiles *138*

Honesty Win a Date with Tad Hamilton! (2nd clip) *172*

Honor Bobby Jones: Stroke of Genius *38*, King Arthur *94*

Hope Elf *62*, The Family Man (2nd clip) *68*, Flight of the Phoenix *72*, The Lord of the Rings: The Two Towers (2nd clip) *100*, Napoleon Dynamite *124*, Say Anything *150*, Win a Date with Tad Hamilton! (2nd clip) *172*

Humanity Spider-Man 2 *160*

Hypocrisy The Passion of the Christ (2nd clip) *130*

Identity The Terminal *166*

Image The Incredibles *88*, Shrek 2 *158*

Impacting others Life as a House *96*

Impossibilities Miracle *112*

Influence Pay It Forward *134*, Radio *140*

Innocence The Passion of the Christ (3rd clip) *132*

Insecurity Bowling for Columbine *40*

Integrity Bobby Jones: Stroke of Genius *38*, My Life (3rd clip) *120*, Saving Private Ryan *148*

Jealousy Envy *64*

Jesus' trial The Passion of the Christ (3rd clip) *132*

Joy About Schmidt *30*, Friday Night Lights *76*

Judging others 50 First Dates *28*, Saved! *146*

Kindness Napoleon Dynamite *124*, Pay It Forward *134*, Radio *140*, Scrooged *154*, Seabiscuit *156*

Knowing someone Win a Date with Tad Hamilton! (1st clip) *170*

Knowledge The Best of Saturday Night Live: Steve Martin *134*

Leadership Napoleon Dynamite *124*

Legacy Antwone Fisher *32*, My Life (1st clip) *116*, Saving Private Ryan *148*, School of Rock *152*

Letting go Cheaper by the Dozen *48*

Lies The Lord of the Rings: The Two Towers (3rd clip) *102*, The Passion of the Christ (2nd clip) *130*, The Sure Thing *164*

Lifestyle Envy *64*

Loneliness Cast Away *44*, How the Grinch Stole Christmas *84*

Longing Win a Date with Tad

9

Hamilton! (2nd clip) *172*
Lord's Prayer Friday Night Lights *76*
Loss Cast Away *44*, Raising Helen *142*, Saving Private Ryan *148*
Love Antwone Fisher *32*, Cast Away *44*, Elf *62*, The Family Man (1st clip) *66*, The Family Man (2nd clip) *68*, Flight of the Phoenix *72*, My Big Fat Greek Wedding *114*, Napoleon Dynamite *124*, Notting Hill *126*, Shrek 2 *158*, The Stepford Wives *162*, The Sure Thing *164*, Win a Date with Tad Hamilton! (1st clip) *170*, Win a Date with Tad Hamilton! (2nd clip) *172*
Loving the unlovable Seabiscuit *156*
Loyalty The Passion of the Christ (1st clip) *128*, The Terminal *166*
Lying Confessions of a Teenage Drama Queen *58*
Mankind Scrooged *154*
Marriage The Family Man (1st clip) *66*, The Family Man (2nd clip) *68*, My Big Fat Greek Wedding *114*
Materialism A Charlie Brown Christmas *46*, A Christmas Story (1st clip) *50*, Jingle All the Way *90*
Maturity Finding Nemo *70*
Meaning of Christmas Jingle All the Way *90*
Media Bowling for Columbine *40*
Men versus women The Stepford Wives *162*
Mercy 50 First Dates *28*, Scrooged *154*
Messiah The Passion of the Christ (3rd clip) *132*
Mission About Schmidt *30*
Mistakes 13 Going on 30 *26*
Moral code Bobby Jones: Stroke of Genius *38*
Morals I, Robot *86*
Motives Jingle All the Way *90*
Names The Terminal *166*
Needs A Christmas Story (1st clip) *50*
Normalcy The Incredibles *88*
Obedience Finding Nemo *70*, The Stepford Wives *162*
Oppression The Village *168*
Overcoming obstacles The Terminal *166*

Panic Bowling for Columbine *40*
Paranoia Bowling for Columbine *40*
Parenting Cheaper by the Dozen *48*
Parents Finding Nemo *70*, Home for the Holidays *80*
Past, the The Village *168*
Patriotism Miracle *112*
Perception My Life (3rd clip) *120*, The Santa Clause *144*
Persecution King Arthur *94*
Perseverance Flight of the Phoenix *72*
Perspective A Cinderella Story *56*, Mean Girls *110*
Pharisees The Passion of the Christ (2nd clip) *130*, The Passion of the Christ (3rd clip) *132*, Saved! *146*
Pleasing others Elf *62*
Political correctness The Best of Saturday Night Live: Steve Martin *34*
Power The Stepford Wives *162*
Powers Mystery Men *122*, The Stepford Wives *162*
Prayer Bruce Almighty *42*, Friday Night Lights *76*, Lost in Translation *104*, My Life (2nd clip) *118*, The Passion of the Christ (1st clip) *128*
Pride Bobby Jones: Stroke of Genius *38*, Finding Nemo *70*, The Joy Luck Club *92*
Priorities Radio *140*
Promise The Terminal *166*
Prophecy The Day After Tomorrow *60*
Providence The Matrix Reloaded *108*
Punishment 50 First Dates *28*
Purpose About Schmidt *30*, Bruce Almighty *42*, A Cinderella Story *56*, Flight of the Phoenix *72*, Life as a House *96*, The Matrix Reloaded *108*, The Passion of the Christ (1st clip) *128*, The Santa Clause *144*, Seabiscuit *156*, Zoolander *174*
Questions Zoolander *174*
Real world Say Anything *150*
Reconciliation Pieces of April *136*
Redemption Mean Girls *110*
Regrets 13 Going on 30 *26*, The Hours *82*
Rejection A Cinderella Story *56*, Notting Hill *126*

Relationships The Sure Thing *164*, Win a Date with Tad Hamilton! (2nd clip) *172*

Religion My Big Fat Greek Wedding *114*

Religious leaders The Passion of the Christ (2nd clip) *130*

Reputation King Arthur *94*

Requests My Life (2nd clip) *118*

Respect Bobby Jones: Stroke of Genius *38*, Freaky Friday *74*, My Life (3rd clip) *120*

Restoration The Lord of the Rings: The Two Towers (1st clip) *98*

Revelation The Day After Tomorrow *60*

Revolution I, Robot *86*

Righteousness Saved! *146*

Risk Notting Hill *126*

Rituals My Big Fat Greek Wedding *114*

Romance The Family Man (1st clip) *66*

Rules I, Robot *86*

Sacrifice Saving Private Ryan *148*, Spider-Man 2 *160*

Salvation Bruce Almighty *42*, Cast Away *44*, Spider-Man 2 *160*

Sanctification Luther *106*

Satan The Lord of the Rings: The Two Towers (3rd clip) *102*, Luther *106*

Savior A Charlie Brown Christmas *46*

Scripture A Charlie Brown Christmas *46*

Selfishness Jingle All the Way *90*, The Joy Luck Club *92*, Planes, Trains, and Automobiles *138*

Selflessness King Arthur *94*, Shrek 2 *158*, Spider-Man 2 *160*

Self-preservation The Passion of the Christ (2nd clip) *130*

Serving others Pay It Forward *134*, Planes, Trains, and Automobiles *138*, School of Rock *152*

Sex The Sure Thing *164*

Sharing Planes, Trains, and Automobiles *138*

Sickness Life as a House *96*

Significance About Schmidt *30*, Mean Girls *110*, My Life (3rd clip) *120*, Zoolander *174*

Sin Cast Away *44*, Hidalgo *78*, The Village *168*

Sin nature The Lord of the Rings: The Two Towers (1st clip) *98*, The Lord of the Rings: The Two Towers (3rd clip) *102*

Soul mate Win a Date with Tad Hamilton! (1st clip) *170*

Sowing and reaping Hidalgo *78*

Stories The Lord of the Rings: The Two Towers (2nd clip) *100*

Strength Pieces of April *136*

Strength in God The Passion of the Christ (1st clip) *128*

Stubbornness Finding Nemo *70*

Submission Notting Hill *126*

Success Cheaper by the Dozen *48*

Suicide The Hours *82*

Surrender Bruce Almighty *42*

Taking a chance Seabiscuit *156*

Taking responsibility The Hours *82*, The Joy Luck Club *92*

Talents Bruce Almighty *42*, Mystery Men *122*, The Santa Clause *144*, School of Rock *152*, Seabiscuit *156*

Teamwork Miracle *112*

Teenage wisdom The Best of Saturday Night Live: Steve Martin *34*

Temptations The Lord of the Rings: The Two Towers (3rd clip) *102*

Ten Commandments I, Robot *86*

Terror Bowling for Columbine *40*

Time The Incredibles *88*, Jingle All the Way *90*

Toys Jingle All the Way *90*

Tradition Antwone Fisher *32*

Transformation The Santa Clause *144*

Treasure Win a Date with Tad Hamilton! (1st clip) *170*

Troubles The Lord of the Rings: The Two Towers (2nd clip) *100*

True love The Santa Clause *144*, Win a Date with Tad Hamilton! (2nd clip) *172*

Trust Big Fish *36*, Friday Night Lights *76*

Truth My Life (1st clip) *116*, The Passion of the Christ (3rd clip) *132*

Turmoil Luther *106*

Ugliness The Santa Clause *144*

Unconfessed sin Lost in Translation *104*

Unity Friday Night Lights *76*,

Miracle *112*
Unworthiness Luther *106*
Urban legend Bowling for Columbine *40*
Value Saving Private Ryan *148*
Values Bobby Jones: Stroke of Genius *38*, Bowling for Columbine *40*, Cheaper by the Dozen *48*, The Family Man (2nd clip) *68*, I, Robot *86*
Victory The Lord of the Rings: The Two Towers (2nd clip) *100*
Vision Seabiscuit *156*
Wants A Christmas Story (2nd clip) *52*

War Saving Private Ryan *148*
Weaknesses Luther *106*
Wisdom The Best of Saturday Night Live: Steve Martin *34*
Wishes A Christmas Story (1st clip) *50*
Worth Mean Girls *110*, My Big Fat Greek Wedding *114*, School of Rock *152*
Wrestling Luther *106*
Wrong versus right The Best of Saturday Night Live: Steve Martin *34*

Quick Clip Locator

BY BIBLE REFERENCE

Genesis

2:18 .... The Family Man (1st clip) 66,
My Big Fat Greek Wedding 114
2:24 .... The Family Man (1st clip) 66,
My Big Fat Greek Wedding 114,
Win a Date with Tad Hamilton!
(2nd clip) 172
6:13 .... The Day After Tomorrow 60
9:11 .... The Day After Tomorrow 60
17:7 .... The Terminal 166

Exodus

20:1-17 .... I, Robot 86
20:12 .... Finding Nemo 70, Freaky Friday 74,
The Joy Luck Club 92
20:17 .... Envy 64

Leviticus

19:15 .... Saved! 146, Seabiscuit 156
21:13 .... Win a Date with
Tad Hamilton! (2nd clip) 172

Numbers

30:2 .... The Terminal 166

Deuteronomy

4:31 .... The Terminal 166
5:16 .... Home for the Holidays 80
6:17 .... I, Robot 86
7:9 .... The Terminal 166
11:1 .... I, Robot 86
15:7 .... Seabiscuit 156
32:4 .... Luther 106
32:7 .... Christmas Vacation 54

Joshua

24:15 .... Cheaper by the Dozen 48

1 Samuel

2:3 .... The Joy Luck Club 92
16:7 .... 13 Going on 30 26, A Cinderella
Story 56, Napoleon Dynamite 124,
Radio 140, Shrek 2 158
16:7b .... Zoolander 174

2 Samuel

11 .... Envy 64

1 Chronicles

29:12 .... Mystery Men 122

2 Chronicles

6:8-9 .... Cheaper by the Dozen 48
7:14 .... Bowling for Columbine 40,
Bruce Almighty 42, Lost in Translation 104
15:7 .... King Arthur 94, Spider-Man 2 160

Ezra

9:13 .... 50 First Dates 28

Esther

4:14 .... The Matrix Reloaded 108
7:1-10 .... The Matrix Reloaded 108

Job

5:2 .... Envy 64
5:11 .... The Terminal 166
36:13 ...... How the Grinch Stole Christmas 84

Psalms

9:18 .... About Schmidt 30
15:1-5 ...... Bobby Jones: Stroke of Genius 38
19:7-8 .... I, Robot 86
25:16 .... Cast Away 44
31:9-10, 14 .... The Hours 82
31:24 .... Miracle 112, Spider-Man 2 160
32:5 .... Envy 64
34:18 .... The Hours 82, Raising Helen 142,
Win a Date with Tad Hamilton!
(2nd clip) 172
37:4 .... A Christmas Story (1st clip) 50,
The Sure Thing 164
37:8 .... Freaky Friday 74
51:6 .... Big Fish 36
56:8 .... Raising Helen 142
56:11 .... Bowling for Columbine 40
59:12 .... Confessions of a Teenage
Drama Queen 58
66:20 .... My Life (2nd clip) 118
68:5 .... Antwone Fisher 32
68:6 ...... Planes, Trains, and Automobiles 138
69:14 .... The Day After Tomorrow 60
72:13 .... About Schmidt 30, Seabiscuit 156
86:15 .... 50 First Dates 28
90:12 .... The Family Man (1st clip) 66
94:19 .... Say Anything 150
103:2-5 .... Seabiscuit 156

103:10 ....50 First Dates *28*
103:12 .... The Village *168*
111:7 ....I, Robot *86*
119:176.............................. Cast Away *44*
121:7 .... The Day After Tomorrow *60*
127:3 ....Cheaper by the Dozen *48*, Elf *62*, Jingle All the Way *90*, My Life (1st clip) *116*
133:1 .... Miracle *112*
139:14-16 .... Freaky Friday *74*, My Life (1st clip) *116*
147:3 .... Pieces of April *136*

Proverbs

1:7 .... The Best of Saturday Night Live: Steve Martin *34*
3:3 ....Pay It Forward *134*
3:5-6 .... Zoolander *174*
3:13-15 .... The Family Man (1st clip) *66*
5:22 .... The Village *168*
6:16, 19 ....Confessions of a Teenage Drama Queen *58*
10:1 .... Home for the Holidays *80*
10:9 .... Bobby Jones: Stroke of Genius *38*
10:12 ......How the Grinch Stole Christmas *84*
10:14 .... The Best of Saturday Night Live: Steve Martin *34*
11:2...............................The Joy Luck Club *92*
11:6 .... The Lord of the Rings: The Two Towers (3rd clip) *102*
11:13 .... My Life (3rd clip) *120*
12:17 .... Big Fish *36*
12:23 .... Big Fish *36*
13:12 ....Notting Hill *126*
14:12 ....Napoleon Dynamite *124*
15:14 .... The Best of Saturday Night Live: Steve Martin *34*
16:3 .... Say Anything *150*
16:9 ....Zoolander *174*
16:18 ....Finding Nemo *70*
16:28 .... Mean Girls *110*
17:6 .... Christmas Vacation *54*
17:17 ....13 Going on 30 *26*, Friday Night Lights *76*, Napoleon Dynamite *124*
18:12 ....Scrooged *154*
18:24 ...... Friday Night Lights *76*, The Lord of the Rings: The Two Towers (2nd clip) *100*, Napoleon Dynamite *124*
19:5 ....Confessions of a Teenage Drama Queen *58*
19:17 ....About Schmidt *30*
19:22 ....Pay It Forward *134*
20:3 ....:... Mean Girls *110*
20:6 ....Napoleon Dynamite *124*, Notting Hill *126*

21:21 ....Notting Hill *126*
22:1 .... My Life (3rd clip) *120*, The Terminal *166*
22:9 ......Planes, Trains, and Automobiles *138*
23:22 .... Home for the Holidays *80*
23:24 ....Elf *62*
25:14 ....Mystery Men *122*
27:6 .... 13 Going on 30 *26*, Napoleon Dynamite *124*
27:17 .... The Lord of the Rings: The Two Towers (2nd clip) *100*
27:19 .....Big Fish *36*, Bobby Jones: Stroke of Genius *38*, Seabiscuit *156*, The Sure Thing *164*
29:15 ....Jingle All the Way *90*
31:10-31 .... The Stepford Wives *162*
31:30 ....13 Going on 30 *26*, Shrek 2 *158*

Ecclesiastes

1:11............................... My Life (3rd clip) *120*
3:1-10 .... Flight of the Phoenix *72*, Life as a House *96*
4:9-10 .... The Lord of the Rings: The Two Towers (2nd clip) *100*, Napoleon Dynamite *124*
6:10 ....The Matrix Reloaded *108*
6:12 .... The Family Man (2nd clip) *68*
7:1 .... My Life (3rd clip) *120*
9:2-3 ....The Matrix Reloaded *108*
9:11............Mystery Men *122*, Seabiscuit *156*
11:8-10.................... Christmas Vacation *54*
11:9............. Big Fish *36*, The Sure Thing *164*
11:10......How the Grinch Stole Christmas *84*, Pieces of April *136*

Song of Songs

2:4 .... Antwone Fisher *32*
7:10 ....Win a Date with Tad Hamilton! (1st clip) *170*, Win a Date with Tad Hamilton! (2nd clip) *172*
8:6 ....Win a Date with Tad Hamilton! (1st clip) *170*

Isaiah

1:17 .... King Arthur *94*
40:8 .... The Best of Saturday Night Live: Steve Martin *34*
43:1 .... The Terminal *166*
43:18 .... The Village *168*
53:6 .... Cast Away *44*

Jeremiah

1:5 .... My Life (1st clip) *116*
1:19 ....The Matrix Reloaded *108*, Saving Private Ryan *148*

29:11-13... Say Anything *150*, Seabiscuit *156*, Zoolander *174*
29:12-13 .... Lost in Translation *104*

Lamentations
3:32 .... Saving Private Ryan *148*

Ezekiel
16:44 .... The Joy Luck Club *92*, Pieces of April *136*

Hosea
2:19-20 .... Win a Date with Tad Hamilton! (2nd clip) *172*
6:6 .... The Passion of the Christ (2nd clip) *130*, The Stepford Wives *162*
10:12 .... Hidalgo *78*

Zechariah
7:9-10 .... Pay It Forward *134*, Radio *140*
7:10 .... About Schmidt *30*

Malachi
2:14-15 .... The Stepford Wives *162*
4:6 .... Elf *62*, Home for the Holidays *80*, The Incredibles *88*, Life as a House *96*, Pieces of April *136*

Matthew
1:18-25 .... A Christmas Story (2nd clip) *52*
5:11..... A Cinderella Story *56*, Confessions of a Teenage Drama Queen *58*
5:33-37 .... The Terminal *166*
5:43-44 .... A Cinderella Story *56*
6:5-6 .... Bruce Almighty *42*, Lost in Translation *104*, My Life (2nd clip) *118*
6:8 .... A Christmas Story (1st clip) *50*
6:14-15 ..... The Hours *82*, Pieces of April *136*
6:19-20 .... A Charlie Brown Christmas *46*
6:25-34 .... Say Anything *150*
6:26 .... A Cinderella Story *56*, School of Rock *152*
6:33 .... Cheaper by the Dozen *48*, The Family Man (2nd clip) *68*
6:34 .... Bruce Almighty *42*
7:7 .... My Life (2nd clip) *118*
10:32-33 ....The Passion of the Christ (2nd clip) *130*
12:7 .... Radio *140*
15:18 .... Big Fish *36*
16:13-20 .... My Life (3rd clip) *120*
16:23 .... Luther *106*
16:24-26 ....Spider-Man 2 *160*

16:26 ....13 Going on 30 *26*, Cheaper by the Dozen *48*
18:18-19 .... My Life (2nd clip) *118*
19:4-6 .... Win a Date with Tad Hamilton! (1st clip) *170*
19:26 ....Pay It Forward *134*
20:30-34 ....Pay It Forward *134*
21:22 ....My Life (2nd clip) *118*
25:21 ....School of Rock *152*
25:37-40 ....About Schmidt *30*
25:40 ....Planes, Trains, and Automobiles *138*
26:28 .... The Hours *82*
26:36-46 ....The Passion of the Christ (1st clip) *128*
26:41 .... The Lord of the Rings: The Two Towers (3rd clip) *102*
26:57-68 ....The Passion of the Christ (2nd clip) *130*
26:69-75 ....The Passion of the Christ (2nd clip) *130*
27:11-25.................The Passion of the Christ (2nd clip) *130*, The Passion of the Christ (3rd clip) *132*
28:19 .... The Day After Tomorrow *60*

Mark
1:4 .... My Big Fat Greek Wedding *114*
1:8 .... My Big Fat Greek Wedding *114*
7:20-23 .... Envy *64*
8:33 ....The Passion of the Christ (1st clip) *128*
10:45 ....The Passion of the Christ (3rd clip) *132*, Spider-Man 2 *160*
10:51 ....Pay It Forward *134*

Luke
1:37 ....Pay It Forward *134*
1:78-79 ....50 First Dates *28*
2:1-20 .... A Charlie Brown Christmas *46*, A Christmas Story (2nd clip) *52*
3:11.......Planes, Trains, and Automobiles *138*
6:22 .... A Cinderella Story *56*
6:36 ....50 First Dates *28*
6:37 .... Saved! *146*
9:48 ....Seabiscuit *156*
11:1-4.............. Friday Night Lights *76*, Lost in Translation *104*, My Life (2nd clip) *118*
11:9-13... Elf *62*
11:13..................... Home for the Holidays *80*, Jingle All the Way *90*
12:1-3 ....Saved! *146*
12:4-5 .... Bowling for Columbine *40*
12:6-7 .... Mean Girls *110*
12:15 .... A Christmas Story (1st clip) *50*,

The Lord of the Rings:
The Two Towers (3rd clip) *102*
12:33 ....Scrooged *154*
12:34 ....A Charlie Brown Christmas *46*,
Jingle All the Way *90*
12:48b ....Mystery Men *122*,
The Santa Clause *144*
14:12-14 .... Planes, Trains, and
Automobiles *138*
15:3-6 .... Cast Away *44*
16:10 .... Bobby Jones: Stroke of Genius *38*
22:39-46 ....The Passion of the Christ
(1st clip) *128*

John
1:17 ....50 First Dates *28*
3:16 .... A Charlie Brown Christmas *46*
4:23-26 ....The Passion of the Christ
(3rd clip) *132*
4:24 ....Confessions of a Teenage
Drama Queen *58*
5:41 ....Confessions of a Teenage
Drama Queen *58*
7:24 ....Shrek 2 *158*
8:43 ....Lost in Translation *104*
12:43 ....Confessions of a Teenage
Drama Queen *58*
13:7 ....Lost in Translation *104*
13:34-35 ....Win a Date with Tad Hamilton!
(1st clip) *170*
13:36-38 ....The Passion of the Christ
(2nd clip) *130*
14:6 ....The Passion of the Christ
(3rd clip) *132*
14:27 .... Say Anything *150*
15:13 .... The Lord of the Rings:
The Two Towers (2nd clip) *100*,
Napoleon Dynamite *124*, Saving
Private Ryan *148*, Spider-Man 2 *160*
16:20 ....Raising Helen *142*
16:33 ....Bowling for Columbine *40*,
King Arthur *94*, The Matrix
Reloaded *108*
18:33-37 ....The Passion of the Christ
(3rd clip) *132*

Acts
2:22-24 ....The Passion of the Christ
(1st clip) *128*

Romans
2:1 ....Saved! *146*
3:23-24 ....50 First Dates *28*
5:18-21 ....50 First Dates *28*
5:3-4 .... Bobby Jones: Stroke of Genius *38*

5:3-5 .... Flight of the Phoenix *72*
5:8 ....Seabiscuit *156*
6:3 .... My Big Fat Greek Wedding *114*
6:14 .... The Lord of the Rings:
The Two Towers (1st clip) *98*
6:22 .... The Lord of the Rings:
The Two Towers (1st clip) *98*
6:23 .... Hidalgo *78*
7:14-25 .... The Lord of the Rings: The Two
Towers (3rd clip) *102*, Luther *106*
8:1 .... The Village *168*
8:2 .... The Lord of the Rings:
The Two Towers (1st clip) *98*, Luther *106*
8:3 .... The Lord of the Rings:
The Two Towers (3rd clip) *102*
8:24-25 .... Flight of the Phoenix *72*
8:28 ....Bruce Almighty *42*, Zoolander *174*
8:35-39 .... Bowling for Columbine *40*,
Cast Away *44*, The Village *168*
11:29...................................Mystery Men *122*
12:2 .... The Santa Clause *144*
12:4-5 .... Cheaper by the Dozen *48*,
Miracle *112*, School of Rock *152*
12:21 .... Hidalgo *78*
13:2 ....Finding Nemo *70*
13:10 ....Radio *140*
13:13 .... The Sure Thing *164*
14:1 .... Big Fish *36*
14:8 .... Life as a House *96*
15:1 ....Mystery Men *122*
15:7 .... Big Fish *36*
16:20 .... Luther *106*

1 Corinthians
1:27-31 ....School of Rock *152*
3:11 .... The Best of Saturday Night Live:
Steve Martin *34*, A Christmas Story
(1st clip) *50*
6:16-20 .... The Sure Thing *164*
7:2 ....Win a Date with Tad Hamilton!
(2nd clip) *172*
7:9 ....Win a Date with Tad Hamilton!
(2nd clip) *172*
7:16 .... My Big Fat Greek Wedding *114*
10:13 .... The Lord of the Rings:
The Two Towers (3rd clip) *102*
10:23-24 ....Finding Nemo *70*
11:3.................Win a Date with Tad Hamilton!
(2nd clip) *172*
12:4 ....School of Rock *152*
12:20 ....Miracle *112*
13:4-7 .... The Family Man (1st clip) *66*,
Freaky Friday *74*, Notting Hill *126*
13:11 .... 13 Going on 30 *26*

13:13 .... Flight of the Phoenix 72,
My Life (1st clip) 116
14:33 ....Lost in Translation 104

2 Corinthians
4:8-9 .... King Arthur 94
5:8-9 .... Elf 62
5:14-15 .... Saving Private Ryan 148
6:14 .... My Big Fat Greek Wedding 114,
Win a Date with Tad Hamilton!
(2nd clip) 172
6:18 .... Elf 62
7:10 .... The Hours 82
9:15 .... A Christmas Story (2nd clip) 52
10:17 .... The Joy Luck Club 92

Galatians
5:14 .... Saving Private Ryan 148,
Shrek 2 158
5:22-23 ....About Schmidt 30,
Pay It Forward 134
6:1 .... Saved! 146

Ephesians
2:8-9 ....50 First Dates 28
3:1-8 .... My Life (1st clip) 116
4:7 .... A Christmas Story (2nd clip) 52
4:7-13 ....School of Rock 152
4:25-27 .... Mean Girls 110
4:26 .... Freaky Friday 74
4:31 ....How the Grinch Stole Christmas 84
4:32 ....The Incredibles 88
5:22 .... The Stepford Wives 162
5:23, 33 .... Win a Date with Tad Hamilton!
(2nd clip) 172
5:25 .... The Stepford Wives 162
5:33 .... My Big Fat Greek Wedding 114
6:1 ....Finding Nemo 70
6:1-4 ....The Incredibles 88
6:2 .... Freaky Friday 74
6:4 .... Elf 62, Finding Nemo 70, Home for
the Holidays 80, My Life (1st clip) 116
6:12 .... Luther 106, Spider-Man 2 160

Philippians
2:1-4 .... Napoleon Dynamite 124, Win a Date
with Tad Hamilton! (1st clip) 170
2:3 .... 13 Going on 30 26, The Family Man
(2nd clip) 68, The Incredibles 88, Jingle
All the Way 90, Mean Girls 110, My Big
Fat Greek Wedding 114, Radio 140,
Scrooged 154, Shrek 2 158
2:12-13 ....School of Rock 152
3:8 ....Notting Hill 126
3:12-14 .... 13 Going on 30 26,

The Village 168
3:20-21 .... The Santa Clause 144
4:6 .... Bruce Almighty 42,
Friday Night Lights 76, Lost in
Translation 104, My Life (2nd clip) 118
4:8 ....The Incredibles 88
4:13 ....Miracle 112

Colossians
1:6 ....The Matrix Reloaded 108
2:6-10 .... Bruce Almighty 42
3:12-14 ....Saved! 146
3:12-14, 17 ....Scrooged 154
3:21 .... Freaky Friday 74
3:25 .... Hidalgo 78

1 Thessalonians
4:3 .... The Sure Thing 164
4:13 ....Raising Helen 142
5:11..Miracle 112

1 Timothy
1:5 .... Bobby Jones: Stroke of Genius 38;
Win a Date with Tad Hamilton!
(2nd clip) 172
3:4 ....The Incredibles 88
4:12 ... The Joy Luck Club   92, Spider-Man 2
5:8 .... Antwone Fisher 32
5:24-25 .... The Village 168
6:17 ....Cheaper by the Dozen 48
6:18 ......Planes, Trains, and Automobiles 138
6:18-19 ....Pay It Forward 134

2 Timothy
1:7 .... The Santa Clause 144
1:8-9 .... Flight of the Phoenix 72
2:1-4 .... Saving Private Ryan 148
4:7 .... King Arthur 94

Titus
2:2-7 .... Antwone Fisher 32
3:3 .... The Lord of the Rings:
The Two Towers (1st clip) 98

Hebrews
2:9 ....The Passion of the Christ (1st clip) 128
4:12 .... The Lord of the Rings:
The Two Towers (1st clip) 98
10:24 .... Miracle 112
10:24-25 ....The Incredibles 88
10:25 .... Christmas Vacation 54
11:1............................ Flight of the Phoenix 72,
The Village 168
11:32-40...................... The Lord of the Rings:
The Two Towers (2nd clip) 100

12:1 .... Hidalgo 78, The Lord of the Rings:
The Two Towers (1st clip) 98
12:28 .... A Cinderella Story 56
13:2 ....About Schmidt 30, Planes, Trains,
and Automobiles 138, Scrooged 154
13:4 ....Win a Date with Tad Hamilton!
(2nd clip) 172
13:5 .... The Family Man (2nd clip) 68
13:7 .... Christmas Vacation 54

James

1:2-3 .... The Lord of the Rings: The
Two Towers (2nd clip) 100, Miracle 112
1:17 .... A Christmas Story (2nd clip) 52,
The Santa Clause 144,
School of Rock 152
3:13-17 .... The Best of Saturday Night Live:
Steve Martin 34
3:14-16 ....Envy 64, How the Grinch Stole
Christmas 84, The Incredibles 88,
Jingle All the Way 90
4:2-3 .... A Christmas Story (1st clip) 50
4:3 ....My Life (2nd clip) 118
4:7 .... Bruce Almighty 42
4:7-8 .... The Lord of the Rings:
The Two Towers (3rd clip) 102
4:14 ....The Family Man (2nd clip) 68,
Life as a House 96
5:15 ....Friday Night Lights 76
5:16 ....Bruce Almighty 42, Envy 64

1 Peter

1:3-8 .... My Life (2nd clip) 118
2:1-3 ....Envy 64
2:21-24 .... The Passion of the Christ
(1st clip) 128
3:1 .... The Stepford Wives 162
3:7 .... The Stepford Wives 162
3:21 ....My Big Fat Greek Wedding 114
4:7 ....The Day After Tomorrow 60
5:5 .... The Incredibles 88
5:8 ....Luther 106

2 Peter

2:19 .... The Lord of the Rings:
The Two Towers (1st clip) 98

1 John

1:9 .... The Hours 82, The Village 168
2:15 .... A Charlie Brown Christmas 46
3:1 ....Antwone Fisher 32, Elf 62
3:16 ....Saving Private Ryan 148
4:18 ....Notting Hill 126
5:4 ....Pay It Forward 134

Revelation

21:4 .... The Day After Tomorrow 60,
Life as a House 96, Raising Helen 142

A quick NEW note from Doug before you read this introduction.

Eddie and I are honored that you chose to use another edition of *Videos that Teach*. Because we know our students are influenced by worldly standards every day, we take great joy in transforming those messages into ministry opportunities relative to youth culture. Based on the overwhelmingly positive feedback we've received from youth workers, we know these books have been helpful for many ministries. Story after story, youth workers tell us that using video clips makes their communication more effective and captivates their students' attention.

Besides the redeeming nature of this book, I know from personal experience that the energy and creativity required for teaching on a regular basis can cause periods of mental fatigue. Ideas that once flowed freely suddenly dry up. The good news is that you have billions of dollars' worth of resources available at your local video store; you don't have to come up with great ideas on your own. This book will help you harness some of the teachable moments you'll find on their shelves.

While we've been using video clips for several years in our ministries, a fairly new technique we've adopted has taken them to a new level. We no longer show the video clip straight from the DVD. We've found that buying inexpensive video-editing software gives us much greater flexibility while also creating a new ministry that teenagers can take part in. Using video software, students can take several different clips and put them together as one video clip. This takes away the need to cue up several videos and completely eliminates the delay between videos.

An added bonus we've found is that we can add black space to the front and back of the clips so they can be cued, fade in nicely, and then finish without showing a still image or turning to static before the stop button is pressed. Sometimes we even use that black space to add introductory words to the clip. One word of caution: if you use students to collect and edit video clips, always preview what they may be watching to make sure it's appropriate—as well as the final result before using it with your group.

As you begin to use this book, you will start to develop a knack for seeing biblical truths in movies not mentioned in this volume. You will become more spiritually sensitive to how God can use what the world meant for secular entertainment for his eternal purposes. While we don't glorify or endorse anything that comes out of Hollywood, we do believe, as the apostle Paul did (Acts 17:16-34), that we can use the understanding of the world and turn it around for good.

There is something wonderful in that moment when students

realize how God's truths can be revealed in culture—whether they learn how God moves in our culture or how lives are damaged by ungodly standards. When there is an understanding that the Bible isn't just a lifeless book but a personal narrative that includes them and speaks to their issues, lives are changed.

It's an honor for me to help you as you weave these narrative moments into your teaching and your students' lives. My prayer is that they will continue to inspire, challenge, and provide opportunities for the students in your church to gain a deeper understanding of the Master Storyteller.

Be careful!

Be wise and preview each clip. Please be sure to read the FAQ: "Why are some clips in this book from R-rated movies?" (page 22)

A DVD idea

One additional suggestion, which we first mentioned in *Videos That Teach 3*, is to use the subtitle option. If you are using DVD players to show the clips, you might want to turn on the subtitles in English. It's a powerful tool. Watching the clip while reading the dialogue is different from students' usual experiences, and it can help drive home a point that you are trying to use in your illustration or message, similar to showing the words of a song as it is played.

What's different about this book? (Important!)

In this book, getting to the actual clip is a little different from the first volume, but the same as in the second and third volumes. **Instead of just putting in the videotape or DVD and having the VCR or DVD player automatically set the counter to zero, you'll need to fast forward to the movie logo. Once you arrive at the movie logo (you'll usually see "This motion picture has been modified to fit your screen," right before the logo), hit "reset" on your counter, and fast-forward to the start time listed in the book.**

One more difference you'll find in *Videos That Teach 4* is the inclusion of holiday-related clip studies. There are 30 clips altogether, covering holidays and special days such as Valentine's Day, Memorial Day, Easter, Independence Day, Halloween, Thanksgiving, Christmas, and others. Talking about the holidays with your students is a great way to help them open up about things they wouldn't normally feel as comfortable discussing, such as family issues.

So there I am, standing before a group of students, teaching a lesson about God's grace that I just knew would be unforgettable (after all, it took several hours to prepare—besides, it was one of those messages that would make my preaching professor proud…if he were still alive).

Halfway through my lesson, two guys in the back row start smacking each other. "Knock it off, jerk!" one of them says loudly.

Of course everyone turns around to see what's happening. I put on my Wounded Puppy Dog/Semi-Stern Pastor's Frown in a desperate attempt to communicate the hurt and disappointment I feel watching these two punks effectively kill the learning experience for everyone in the room. At the same time, four girls near the front put their heads together and whisper something to each other. A guy slouching in the middle of the room yells out, "Hey, Doug, when will this sermon be over?" Then a girl from the whispering quartet runs out of the room crying.

So much for the unforgettable lesson about grace. My mind shifts to law, and I imagine sacrificing a few students on the altar of my frustration. I vow never to teach students again.

Yet within 48 hours, the memories of yet another hellfest begin fading. I repress the pain of failure and begin looking (again) for fresh ways to teach next week from God's Word. Although inevitably a journey of pain and privilege, it's a journey that can be made a little easier by the book you're now holding.

Esther, Everyman, and Ever After

The ancient Hebrews told patriarchal stories. Jesus told parables. The medieval church staged morality plays. And Hollywood has become our culture's premier storyteller. Stories—whether read, recited, or enacted—have always gripped people's imaginations and emotions. Movies are today's parables. Theater attendance is at a record high, multiplexes are being built everywhere, and the movie industry is making more money than ever before. Even if these facts make you wince, you can still see how *Videos That Teach 4* uses movies—that is, visual storytelling—to launch meaningful discussions that go beyond the surface of the script to kids' spirits, discussions that get kids talking about themselves and life and God.

Why use movie clips in youth meetings, anyway?

Many of your students are visual learners—which means they'll be impacted more by seeing a message than by merely hearing it. And whether we like it or not, that's how most students seem to be learning these days, living in a culture saturated with visual media. An incessant, 24-hour stream of images on video, TV, movies, and the Internet surround us. Teenagers tend to be very comfortable with it all and respond well to it.

Which is why video makes perfect sense if you want to grab your students' attention.

And clips from videotaped movies are among those visual tools. For years Doug used object lessons, "spontaneous melodramas," and a variety of other creative teaching methods to reinforce his Bible teaching. He always wanted to use video clips but could never remember the right movie at the right time for the right message. His teaching changed when Eddie James joined him at Saddleback Church. Eddie—whose mind is a virtual storehouse of movie and video clips—would do a quick mental search on the topic Doug was to speak on and invariably come up with a clip to use. That gift of Eddie's quickly improved Doug's teaching and the students' interest.

FAQs

• **What about the copyright law?**
Motion pictures are fully protected by copyright. Public exhibition, especially when an admission fee is charged, could violate copyright. The copyright doctrine of fair use, however, permits certain uses of brief excerpts from copyrighted materials for not-for-profit teaching purposes without permission. If you have specific questions about whether your plans to use film clips or other copyrighted materials in your lessons are permissible under these guidelines, you should consult your church's legal counsel. Or you or your church could apply for a blanket licensing agreement from The Motion Picture Licensing Corporation (*www.mplc.org*) for about $100 per year.

• **Why are some clips in this book from R-rated movies?***
Because none of the clips in *Videos That Teach 4*, even those from R-rated movies (unless noted) contain language or content that is inappropriate or questionable to most youth groups.

Because clips from R movies evoke very intense emotions and imagery.

Because sometimes, carefully, you can teach good theology by pointing to bad theology.

Because of course you'll preview whatever clip you want to use to make sure it's appropriate for your lesson and for your group.

Because if, after you've previewed it, you're still unsure if it's suitable, you can always show it to your pastor, supervisor, or a

*Here are the 9 movies: *About Schmidt, Bowling for Columbine, The Joy Luck Club, Life as a House, Lost in Translation, The Matrix Reloaded, The Passion of the Christ, Planes, Trains, and Automobiles, Saving Private Ryan.*

parent for an opinion.

Because if you still don't feel comfortable using any of this book's 9 clips from R movies, there are still 66 clips that are G, PG, or PG-13.

Because movie ratings are assigned by the dozen or so members on the ratings board of the Motion Picture Association of America—www.mpaa.org—and the board's rating decisions are entirely subjective. The ratings board doesn't base its decisions on scriptural standards of conduct or art. Ratings simply advise viewers about the level of "adult" content in a movie so parents can exercise appropriate control over what their underage children see.

You get the point. The use of a clip in this book does not imply endorsement of—

- The movie in general;
- Other scenes in that movie in particular;
- The actors' lifestyles;
- The use of animals, firearms, or Scripture quotations in the movie; OR
- The manufacturer of the cars used in the chase scenes.
- Etc., etc.

In short, we're not endorsing anything. This book simply lists 75 short clips, most of which (but not all of which) are appropriate and instructive to most youth groups (but not all youth groups) in most situations (but not all situations).

So you make the call. You're an adult. You're a leader of your youth group's teenagers. You know at what point instruction becomes distraction—for you, for your students, for their parents, for your church or organization. Use the summaries—and preview the clip before the lesson!—to discern which movie clips are too sophisticated for your middle schoolers or too elementary for your senior highers. There's a lot to choose from here. Just think before you punch the play button.

- ***Are you sure I need to preview a clip before showing it?***
  If you don't preview a clip, you're asking for trouble—at the least it may cause you embarrassment, and at the most it may cost you your job. As you probably know, youth workers lose their jobs due to oversights like this. Protect yourself, preview the clip, and cue it up precisely.

Illustrating or building a lesson with *Videos That Teach 4*

Most youth workers use this book one of two ways:

• *You already have a lesson and want a clip to illustrate it.* Great. Just flip to the "Quick Clip Locator—by topic" on page 7, find your topic, then turn to the corresponding clip. (If you're a browser, just leaf through the book with an eye on the upper-right corners of the page spreads, where the topics of each clip are listed.) Or if your lesson is based on a Bible passage instead of a topic, check out the "Quick Clip Locator—by Bible reference" on page 13.

• *You simply want a change of pace in this week's youth meeting—and a movie-based lesson sounds good.* See the alphabetical list of movies in the table of contents for a movie you know and like, or just browse through the book until you find a clip that catches your interest.

What you'll find with each clip

Each of the 75 clip outlines in *Videos That Teach 4* contains the same parts, clip to clip. Use as many or as few of the parts as you need to take your lesson where you want it to go. You can use just the clip to illustrate your own lesson...you can build a full-blown Bible study around the clip with the Scripture references provided (and with preliminary study on your part!)...you can trigger small-group discussions with any of several questions provided for each clip (with considerably less preparation). You know your students, so adapt or scavenge accordingly to meet their needs.

Here are the parts each clip outline includes:

Trailer

This is the leading question or statement that gets kids' minds moving down the track of your topic (which are listed, by the way, in the upper-right corner of the first page of each clip's two-page spread). It gives you and your students an idea of what to watch and listen for as you view the clip.

For example, if you just jump into the clip, all you'll get are students reacting to the outcome—without paying attention to the source. On the other hand, if you set up your teaching time with a provocative question, students will still probably laugh at the clip— but underneath their laughter they'll get the point you're making. In fact, depending on how talkative a group you have, this opening question may trigger 15 or 20 minutes of discussion before you ever get to showing the clip.

The movie

If you're not familiar with a movie, this very brief summary helps you out. Even if you do know the movie, you can use (or read aloud) the summary to explain the storyline before you show a clip.

For a thorough, detailed description of the movie, get on the Web, type movie reviews into your favorite search engine, and choose one of the dozens of movie databases available. We found *www.empireonline.co.uk/reviews* particularly helpful. And *www.screenit. com* contains "entertainment reviews for parents" of videos (and movies, music, and DVDs) that not only summarize plot, but also list in detail why the movie received its rating, with categories such as violence, alcohol/drugs, guns/weapons, blood/gore, disrespectful/ bad attitude, sex/nudity, imitative behavior, topics to talk about, and so on.

This clip

With this detailed description of the clip itself, we've also listed the start and stop times of the clip. Simply fast-forward to the movie logo (you'll usually see "This motion picture has been modified to fit your screen" right before the movie logo), reset your counter to zero, and fast-forward to the time where the clip begins. In case either the rental DVD or your DVD player is different from ours, we've also included prompts from the movie—dialogue snippets or scene descriptions—to ensure that you start and stop it at the right time.

By the Book

The Bible is where you want your students to end up, sooner or later. If sooner, here's where you'll find Scripture passages relevant to the clip's topic—use them to build a lesson from scratch or to offer biblical input or to give some direction for small-group discussions.

Where to take it

Here are several discussion questions that generally try to bring together the clip's main point with its relevant Bible passages. Let the questions guide you, not coerce you. Tailor the questions to match the direction you want to take or guide the depth of discussion your kids are capable of. This is the time to help them explore the meanings behind the clip, how the Bible speaks to that particular situation, and how it all applies to them.

Keep on teaching!

25

13 Going on 30

Trailer

Fast-forward your life
17 years from now

The movie Comedy, Rated PG-13

After reading an article called "30, Flirty & Thriving" in *Poise* (her favorite magazine), young Jenna Rink (Jennifer Garner) believes the article's subtitle is true: "The 30s are the best years of your life." So when Jenna's plans to break into the popular crowd at her thirteenth birthday party turn sour, she makes a desperate and tearful wish to jump ahead to her thirties and leave all the teen angst behind. Thanks to a sprinkling of wishing dust, the next day she awakens right in the middle of such a life. Even though Jenna feels like it's only the day after her party, she's actually jumped ahead 17 years into her future. She tracks down her best friend Matt (Mark Ruffalo) to help her make sense of this strange new reality, only to discover he's no longer a part of her life. The more Jenna learns about the last 17 years and the life she now leads as a 30-year-old magazine editor at *Poise*, the more she realizes she must face the consequences of decisions she made long ago.

This clip (about 6 1/2 minutes)

▶ **Start** / 0:54:00 / "I still can't believe you're getting married."

■ **Stop** / 1:00:41 / "I'm sorry I missed last Christmas."

As Jenna becomes aware of the person she has become, one thing is clear: while she got everything she wished for that night in the closet, she didn't understand what the bigger picture might look like once such a request is granted. Feeling lost and alone, Jenna returns to her childhood home. Her mom (Kathy Baker) fixes Jenna her favorite breakfast and the two talk about regrets and what to do about them.

By the Book

1 Samuel 16:7; Proverbs 17:17, 27:6, 31:30; Matthew 16:26; 1 Corinthians 13:11; Philippians 2:3, 3:12-14

Where to take it

? Have you ever done anything to a friend that is similar to what Jenna did to Matt? What happened with that friendship?

? If you were given one do-over—anything in your life—what would it be?

? Have you ever made such a big mistake that it changed your whole life? Share what happened, if you feel comfortable doing so.

? Jenna's mom says she has no regrets, even with her mistakes. Do you see things the way Jenna's mom does? Explain.

? What regrets do you have about your past choices or actions?

? What if you were to wake up one morning and discover that your decisions had taken you away from the person you were meant to be? What would you do?

? If you could travel in time, as Jenna does, would you travel to the future or to the past? Why?

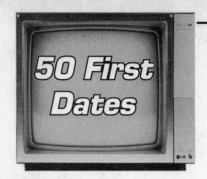

50 First Dates

Trailer
To whom do you need
to show mercy?

The movie   Comedy, Rated PG-13

Lucy (Drew Barrymore) lost her short-term memory after she was in a car accident. When she wakes up each morning, anything that has happened to her since just before the accident is no longer a part of her memory. Henry (Adam Sandler) is a charming marine veterinarian who loves romancing ladies, but only for the short term. Meeting Lucy makes Henry rethink his playboy lifestyle, and he begins spending each day trying to make Lucy fall in love with him all over again.

This clip (1 minute)

▶ **Start** / 0:43:15 / "Okay, this is her. Start beating me up."

■ **Stop** / 0:44:15 / "Sorry. I'm in a community watch program." (Note: Stop immediately after Lucy says this—there's a swear word in the next sentence.)

Henry tries various methods to get Lucy to notice him. One day Henry asks his friend Ula (Rob Schneider) to help him get Lucy's attention as he waits by the side of the road Lucy takes to get home.

By the Book

Ezra 9:13; Psalm 86:15, 103:10; Luke 1:78-79, 6:36; John 1:17; Romans 3:23-24, 5:18-21; Ephesians 2:8-9

Where to take it

? What is your definition of *grace*? Of *mercy*?

? Read Psalm 86:15, John 1:17, and Romans 5:18-21. What does the Bible say about grace and mercy? How are they different from one another?

? Who are the people in your life to whom you offer grace or mercy easily? To whom is it more challenging for you to offer these things?

? Describe a time in your life when you were treated with mercy, even though you didn't deserve it. Describe a time when someone showed you grace.

? What does it take for you to be able to ignore people's faults, look beyond their actions, and treat them with love? What would make this easier to do?

? How can you bring grace and mercy into others' lives?

? Henry yells to Lucy that Ula has learned his lesson, but Lucy replies, "Not enough." Is there anyone whom you judge too harshly and essentially say, "Not enough"?

? How about you? Do you beat yourself up about anything? How can you show grace to yourself?

About Schmidt

Has your life made a
difference to someone?

The movie Drama, Rated R

Following his retirement and the sudden death of his wife, Warren Schmidt (Jack Nicholson) finds himself at a crossroads in his life. Uncertain about both his future and his past, he packs up his Winnebago and sets out on a journey to Denver, Colorado, to try to convince his estranged daughter, Jeannie (Hope Davis), not to get married. When every step he takes seems to go wrong, Warren wonders if he is destined to end his life as he lived it: without significance.

This clip (about 6 minutes)

▶ **Start** / 1:53:40 / "Dear Ndugu..."

■ **Stop** / 2:00:00 / Scene fades as Warren is smiling and crying.

Just after his retirement, Warren begins sponsoring a poor Tanzanian boy named Ndugu. Through numerous letters to the boy, Warren recounts his journeys and shares his observations about his life. When Warren returns home from his trip, discouraged about what he has done with his life and his failure to prevent his daughter's wedding, a letter from Tanzania brings him new hope.

By the Book

Psalm 9:18, 72:13; Proverbs 19:17; Zechariah 7:10; Matthew 25:37-40;
Galatians 5:22-23; Hebrews 13:2

Where to take it

? How did this scene affect you? What thoughts or emotions came to
mind?

? Before reading Ndugu's letter, Warren wonders if he's made a difference
with his life. How do you want to make a difference in others' lives? In
the world around you?

? What does it mean to be a world changer? What part of the world has
been made better because of you?

? In what ways is God going to use your gifts and talents for the
betterment of this world?

? In what ways does Ndugu's letter make you want to help the less
fortunate?

? What does the Bible say in Proverbs 19:17 and Zechariah 7:10 about the
poor and the hungry? How can you make a difference to them?

? How can helping others change the way we view our own
circumstances?

Antwone Fisher
(Thanksgiving)

Trailer

Gather around the table
with family

The movie Drama, Rated PG-13

Antwone Fisher (Derek Luke) is on the verge of being kicked out of the Navy because he cannot control his anger. After a fight with a man who outranks him, Fisher is placed on restriction and sent to Dr. Jerome Davenport (Denzel Washington) for an evaluation. Davenport doesn't allow Antwone to breeze through their sessions; he wants to uncover the roots of the young man's violent behavior. At first, Fisher is wary of digging up his past, but he soon begins to trust the doctor, confiding in him the truth about the death of his father, being abandoned by his mother, and the abuses he endured in his foster family. At Davenport's urging, Antwone travels back to Cleveland to see if he can find his family and get answers to some of the questions that have left him unsettled.

This clip (about 3 minutes)

▶ **Start** /1:47:32 / A car drives up the street.

⬛ **Stop** /1:50:22 / "You want some pancakes?"

After making many phone calls in search of his father's family, Antwone makes contact with his father's sister. He goes to her house and, during their conversation, discovers that his mother is living close by. Antwone takes the opportunity to meet her. Although he doesn't get the answers to his questions about why she walked away, he does tell his mother about the man he has become and how he's always wanted to be a part of her life. When Antwone returns to his aunt's house, he is greeted by a number of relatives he's never met before. After a lifetime of feeling alone and abandoned, he's finally welcomed to feast at the table with his real family.

By the Book

Psalm 68:5; Song of Songs 2:4; 1 Timothy 5:8; Titus 2:2-7; 1 John 3:1

Where to take it

- What are your memories of Thanksgiving holidays spent with your family?

- Name some action words that describe your family time on Thanksgiving.

- What kinds of foods are served in your family's Thanksgiving meal? Do any of these dishes hold any traditional value?

- As you watch the doors swing open and Antwone finds himself surrounded by family and food, how does it make you think of heaven?

- Which relationships in your family can sometimes make family gatherings awkward or difficult?

- What does the Bible say in Titus 2:2-7 about families and the way they should treat each other?

The Best of Saturday Night Live: Steve Martin
(Independence Day)

How much history do you know?

The movie   Comedy, Rated PG-13

Steve Martin has been asked to guest host *Saturday Night Live* more than any other person since the show began. The producers of *Saturday Night Live* have put Steve's best bits on a DVD that captures some of Martin's most memorable moments on *SNL* over the last three decades. The collection highlights what the comedian does so well: making people laugh.

This clip   (about 6 minutes)

▶ **Start** / 0:34:00 / "Hello, and welcome to Common Knowledge."

■ **Stop** / 0:40:24 / "Goodnight, everybody."

Steve Martin plays the host of a game show called *Common Knowledge*. This *Jeopardy* rip-off includes an interesting twist to the rules, which rattles the sensibilities of one famous contestant, Jean Kirkpatrick (Nora Dunn), former Ambassador to the United Nations. The reigning champion (Kevin Nealon), who happens to be a high school counselor, doesn't seem to have any problems with the unusual format. Things go from bad to worse for Ms. Kirkpatrick when she must team up with a high school senior (Dana Carvey) for the show's version of a lightning round. Welcome to *Common Knowledge*, where it's not what you know but what you *think* you know.

**history, teenage wisdom,
wrong versus right,
political correctness,
knowledge, wisdom**

By the Book

Proverbs 1:7, 10:14, 15:14; Isaiah 40:8; 1 Corinthians 3:11; James 3:13-17

Where to take it

? If you were on a game show about world history and other facts, how much would you know?

? Do you think teenagers today are interested in the history of our country? Explain.

? Looking ahead to the next 10 to 20 years, do you see teenagers drifting further away from knowledge about things like the Bill of Rights, the Emancipation Proclamation, and the U.S. Constitution? Why or why not?

? How can history teachers inspire teenagers to be more interested in the past?

? Read 1 Corinthians 3:11. What does the Bible say about our foundation?

? How does the history of the Bible play a part in your life? Would you say it's your foundation?

? Though the clip makes us laugh at the players' lack of knowledge, is it true that we sometimes take our freedoms for granted? Why do you think that is?

Big Fish

Trailer

Is it possible to show people
who we really are?

The movie Drama, Rated PG-13

Edward Bloom (Albert Finney) has been telling tall tales for most of his life
and *nearly* everyone he has ever met has been charmed by his larger-than-life
anecdotes. Unfortunately Ed's stories have had the opposite effect on his only
son, Will (Billy Crudup). Frustrated by his father's fondness for exaggeration,
Will hasn't spoken to him in three years. When Will learns that his father is
dying, he returns home to try to find the man behind the myths.

This clip (about 3 1/2 minutes)

▶ **Start** / 1:16:55 / The family is eating breakfast.

■ **Stop** / 1:20:30 / Will leaves the room.

Edward attempts to launch into one of his notorious stories while the family is
eating breakfast. Will interrupts his father and explains how Ed's exaggerations
have made it impossible for Will to trust him. The conversation only widens
the gap between father and son, as neither can accept the other one for who
he really is.

By the Book

Psalm 51:6; Proverbs 12:17, 12:23, 27:19; Ecclesiastes 11:9; Matthew 15:18; Romans 14:1, 15:7

Where to take it

(?) Do you know someone who tells tall tales? What's it like to be around that person?

(?) Why do you think people exaggerate the truth?

(?) What are some things that make it difficult to trust someone?

(?) Ed asks Will, "Who do you want me to be?" In what areas of your life do you feel that you have to be someone different from who you are?

(?) Do you think it is possible to truly show someone who you are? Explain.

(?) Do you think we still accept people after they've shown us their true colors? Explain.

(?) Read Romans 14:1 and 15:7. What does the Bible teach us about acceptance? How can we apply that to our lives?

The movie Drama, Rated PG

In the year 1930, golf's best amateur was also the world's greatest champion. The only player to win all four of golf's major tournaments in one year, Bobby Jones (James Caviezel) overcame his temper, numerous health problems, and family pressures to achieve his amazing record—all by the age of 28. Never accepting a dime of prize money or endorsements, Jones played strictly for the love of the game and spent his life reminding people that the word *amateur* comes from the Latin word for *love*.

This clip (about 2 minutes)

▶ **Start** / 1:18:58 / "Who's better than us?"

■ **Stop** / 1:20:58 / "There are things finer than winning championships."

In a tight final round of the U.S. Open Tournament, Bobby Jones is paired with another of the era's top players, Walter Hagan (Jeremy Northam). While preparing for a shot, Bobby causes his ball to move. Because no one sees the infraction, the tournament official leaves the decision up to Bobby: take the penalty or play through.

By the Book

Psalm 15:1-5; Proverbs 10:9, 27:19; Luke 16:10; Romans 5:3-4;
1 Timothy 1:5

Where to take it

? If you were in Bobby Jones' shoes—if everyone gave you the go-ahead to skip the penalty—would you? Explain. (Be honest—no churchy answers.)

? Describe a time in your life when you were in a tough situation where you could have gotten away with something but your heart was telling you to do the right thing.

? What does the term moral compass mean to you?

? In Luke 16:10, Jesus talks about the importance of being faithful in the little things. How do the little things matter when it comes to character? What are the little things in your life?

? What are some of the most important character traits listed in the Bible? Of these traits, which ones do you think you possess? Which ones would you like to add to your life?

? How do the hard times we go through shape the people we become?

? Describe the impact your most difficult circumstances have had on your character.

Bowling for Columbine

Do we create our own fear?

The movie Documentary, Rated R

This film follows filmmaker Michael Moore as he travels the country asking a few questions: *Why is America so gun-crazy? Why are we so afraid of each other? Why do gun-related crimes in America greatly outnumber those in other developed countries?* Using the school shootings at Littleton, Colorado, as a backdrop, Moore and his film crew search for the answers.

This clip (about 3 minutes)

▶ **Start** / 0:55:50 / Scene shows a button that says THIS HOME IS PREPARED.

■ **Stop** / 0:58:54 / Scene dissolves on woman preparing to defend herself.

This segment presents an assortment of news clips reporting "dangerous" things in the world around us. Moore gives his perspective of how much the media plays a part in teaching us to be fearful of everything from killer bees to Halloween candy.

media, fear, insecurity,
paranoia, terror, 9-11,
panic, values, urban legend

By the Book

2 Chronicles 7:14; Psalm 56:11; Luke 12:4-5; John 16:33; Romans 8:35-39

Where to take it

? How does the media affect what Americans think is important?

? After watching this scene, what other news reports have made you fearful?

? How do we create our own fear?

? Name an urban legend (like the story about the razor blades in the apples) that was blown out of proportion but ultimately untrue.

? As believers, what is our responsibility regarding the words we use when we're talking to others?

? How do we create safe, stable communities when there seems to be so much hatred and terrorism?

? How has 9-11 changed your life? Your outlook on life?

? What aspects of our society have not changed since 9-11?

Bruce Almighty

Have you felt the power of
prayer and surrender?

The movie Comedy, Rated PG-13

Bruce Nolan (Jim Carrey) feels like everyone, including God, is out to get him. Bruce is a television reporter in Buffalo, New York, who resents being assigned to silly community interest stories when his ambition is to be a serious anchor. His dissatisfaction with his life is not only pouring onto his coworkers, but is also ruining his relationship with his girlfriend, Grace (Jennifer Aniston). On a particularly bad day, Bruce loses the anchor job to his rival, gets fired, takes a beating while trying to stop a robbery, and wrecks his car. At the end of his rope, Bruce rails against God for the unfairness of his life and accuses God of not being able to handle things on Earth. God (Morgan Freeman) responds by bestowing his powers upon Bruce—giving Bruce the opportunity to see if he can do a better job. Bruce uses his new clout to right all the wrongs in his own life, but it isn't long before he realizes his attempts at being the Almighty have actually created more chaos in his life and in the lives of those around him.

This clip (about 6 minutes)

▶ **Start** / 1:23:40 / "You know what I do before I go to bed?"

■ **Stop** / 1:29:35 / "You're lucky to be alive, son. Someone up there must like you."

Grace decides she needs to end her relationship with Bruce. So her sister, Debbie (Lisa Ann Walter), stops by Grace and Bruce's apartment to pick up some of Grace's things. Bruce learns from Debbie that Grace has been praying for him extensively. So he listens in as Grace lifts him up to God, and what he discovers finally leads him to surrender. Bruce realizes he doesn't want to be God anymore. So he gets another chance to talk with God about his life, his purpose, and what it means to pray.

By the Book

2 Chronicles 7:14; Matthew 6:5-6, 6:34; Romans 8:28; Philippians 4:6; Colossians 2:6-10; James 4:7, 5:16

Where to take it

❓ What does Matthew 6:5-6 say about prayer?

❓ What do Matthew 6:34 and James 4:7 say about surrender?

❓ If you feel comfortable doing so, share something you've been thinking and praying a lot about recently.

❓ Have you been praying for something or someone other than yourself?

❓ Which of those prayers have been answered, and how?

❓ Bruce declares he doesn't want to "play God" anymore. What are some ways that you play God in your own life?

❓ Bruce's last prayer was real, authentic, and from his heart. In what ways do we make prayer "churchy"?

Cast Away

Ever feel like you've drifted out
of the reach of God's love?

The movie   Adventure/Drama, Rated PG-13

Working for Fed Ex, Chuck Noland (Tom Hanks) is a man driven by the clock. On Christmas Eve, Chuck is called away on a business trip. He tells his fiancé (Helen Hunt) that he will be right back and boards a cargo plane that crashes hours later in the waters of the Pacific Ocean. The sole survivor of the crash, Chuck washes up on a remote island where, for the first time in his life, he is completely alone—all he has is time.

This clip   (about 3 1/2 minutes)

▶ **Start** / 1:40:40 / Shot of the ocean from Chuck's manmade boat.

■ **Stop** / 1:44:08 / "Wilson, Wilson!"

Chuck builds a makeshift raft in an attempt to get off the island. With him on the raft is Wilson, a volleyball that washed ashore on the island and has since become Chuck's best friend and confidant. Days into the voyage, a sun-weary Chuck awakens to find that Wilson has been jostled from the raft and is drifting out to sea and out of Chuck's reach.

By the Book

Psalm 25:16, 119:176; Isaiah 53:6; Luke 15:3-6; Romans 8:35-39

Where to take it

? Do you ever feel like Wilson—like you've floated past the reach of God's love? Share what that was like, if you feel comfortable doing so.

? Describe a time when you felt abandoned by God, only to realize that it was you who had wandered.

? Describe a time when you drifted away and then rediscovered God's love.

? What would you say to someone who wants to just float away from God? Have you ever felt that way?

? What could make someone want to give up on her faith?

? Is there anything you could do on this earth that would cause God to turn his hand, or his face, away from you? Have you ever felt that you didn't deserve God's love?

? Read Romans 8:35-39. What does the Bible say about God's love for us?

A Charlie Brown Christmas
(Christmas)

Trailer
The real meaning of Christmas

The movie Animation, Rated G

Charlie Brown believes the real message of Christmas has been lost and forgotten. He is saddened by how the holiday has become commercialized—his sister, Sally, is asking Santa for cash, and even Snoopy has entered his doghouse in the neighborhood Christmas lighting and display contest. In an attempt to help Charlie overcome his holiday blues, Lucy suggests he get involved with the community Christmas play. Because Christmas is so meaningful to him, Charlie Brown tries to rally the group to put on the best production ever. Unfortunately, the cast is not about to listen to him. Lucy takes over and gives Charlie Brown a new task: find just the right Christmas tree for the stage.

This clip (about 4 1/2 minutes)

- ▶ **Start** / 0:20:20 / "I guess you were right, Linus, I shouldn't have picked this little tree."

- ■ **Stop** / 0:25:00/ The Peanuts gang starts singing "Hark! The Herald Angels Sing."

Charlie Brown presents the little tree to the rest of the gang, which only results in their laughter at the tree's pitiful appearance. Charlie Brown laments that maybe he doesn't know what Christmas is all about and asks if anyone else remembers what it means. Linus (voiced by Christopher Shea) steps to center stage and recites a passage from the Bible, which tells about the birth of Christ. Charlie Brown takes his hapless little tree back home, and as the gang pitches in to decorate it, they're all reminded of the true meaning of Christmas.

By the Book

Matthew 6:19-20; Luke 2:1-20, 12:34; John 3:16; 1 John 2:15

Where to take it

- What are your family's Christmas traditions?

- What values have your parents instilled in you about Christmas? What aspects of Christmas are most important to your family?

- What did Christmas mean to you when you were a child?

- What does it mean to you now?

- Was there ever a year that money was tight and you weren't able to give each other much for Christmas? What do you remember most about that year?

- How will you celebrate Christmas when you have a family of your own?

- Read the story of Jesus' birth in Luke 2:1-20. What are some things about this story that you never realized before?

Cheaper by the Dozen
(Father's Day)

Trailer

What is success in the world really worth if there is failure at home?

The movie Comedy, Rated PG

Tom (Steve Martin) and Kate (Bonnie Hunt) Baker have become accustomed to juggling the responsibilities of raising 12 children. But when Tom is given the opportunity to coach college football at his alma mater, the whole family is turned upside down. Tom struggles to find balance between the demands of his new job and the demands of fatherhood. In the midst of the chaos, Kate learns that her manuscript is being published, and she is swept off on a whirlwind book tour. A string of catastrophes follows as the Baker clan tries to adapt to their new lifestyle.

This clip (about 3 minutes)

▶ **Start** / 1:27:00 / Tom looks at his college yearbook.

■ **Stop** / 1:30:12 / Tom hugs his family.

Tom's boss gives him an ultimatum, forcing him to evaluate what really matters—the job or his family. Although this coaching job has been a dream of Tom's for most of his life, he chooses to resign. When the kids hear about the sacrifice he's making for them, they show up after his final football game with their hearts overflowing with love for Coach.

By the Book

Joshua 24:15; 2 Chronicles 6:8-9; Psalm 127:3; Matthew 6:33, 16:26; Romans 12:4-5; 1 Timothy 6:17

Where to take it

Do you think it's important to pursue your dreams? Is there ever a point when it's time to let go of a dream?

Do you think dreams can change?

How do you define success?

Is it possible to juggle the demands of a family and a career? Explain.

Do you think it's a burden or a blessing to have children?

What advantages and disadvantages do you see in being part of a large family?

Would you prefer to be part of a small family or a large family? Explain.

As a believer, we are also part of a church family. How can you build strong relationships with your brothers and sisters in Christ?

A Christmas Story
(Christmas)

Do you believe in Santa Claus?

The movie Comedy, Rated PG

Ralphie Parker (Peter Billingsley) is a boy who lives with his quirky family in an Indiana suburb in the 1940s. The holidays are just around the corner and Ralphie has his heart set on getting a Red Ryder BB gun for Christmas. Unfortunately every adult in his life thinks that if he were to receive such a present, he would only "shoot his eye out." He'll do whatever he has to do to convince his parents, his teacher, and even a grumpy department store Santa that he can handle such a gift.

This clip (about 6 minutes)

▶ **Start** / 1:05:28 / "There he is!"

■ **Stop** / 1:11:50 / "Merry Christmas." Scene dissolves to black.

No one will accept Ralphie's idea that a Red Ryder air rifle will make the perfect Christmas gift. So as a last-ditch effort, he heads to the mall to talk with Santa (Jeff Gillen) himself. Because the line of children who are waiting to see Saint Nick is so long, Ralphie has plenty of time to prepare what he'll say when it's finally his turn to sit on Santa's lap. But when his big moment arrives—Ralphie freezes up.

By the Book

Psalm 37:4; Matthew 6:8; Luke 12:15; 1 Corinthians 3:11; James 4:2-3

Where to take it

- **?** Did you believe in Santa when you were little?

- **?** Do you think allowing kids to believe in Santa Claus detracts from the true meaning of Christmas? Explain.

- **?** When you have your own family, do you plan to continue the Santa Claus tradition?

- **?** When you were a kid, what were some of the things you asked Santa to bring you?

- **?** When did Christmas "change" for you?

- **?** Why do you think we were more eager to talk with Santa than we are to talk with God today?

- **?** In what ways do we treat God like he's our own personal Santa Claus?

A Christmas Story

(Christmas)

Trailer

Christmas morning?

The movie Comedy, Rated PG

Ralphie Parker (Peter Billingsley) is a boy who lives with his quirky family in an Indiana suburb in the 1940s. The holidays are just around the corner and Ralphie has his heart set on getting a Red Ryder BB gun for Christmas. Unfortunately every adult in his life thinks that if he were to receive such a present, he would only "shoot his eye out." He'll do whatever he has to do to convince his parents, his teacher, and even a grumpy department store Santa that he can handle such a gift.

This clip (9 minutes)

▶ **Start** / 1:14:06 / Ralphie wakes up in his bed.

■ **Stop** / 1:23:08 / "Ralphie, you be careful out there. Don't shoot your eye out!"

Ralphie wakes up with excitement and wonder on Christmas morning. The stage is set perfectly: a white blanket of snow covers the ground and dozens of wrapped gifts wait under the tree downstairs. The only question that remains to be answered is whether or not the present he's been pining for is somewhere under that tree.

By the Book

Matthew 1:18-25; Luke 2:1-20; 2 Corinthians 9:15; Ephesians 4:7;
James 1:17

Where to take it

? What's one of the funniest gifts you've ever received?

? What's one of the most disappointing gifts you've ever received?

? What are some of the best parts of Christmas for your family?

? Read the real Christmas story in Luke 2:1-20. What was happening on this morning?

? Describe a time when you wanted something for Christmas that your parents thought was either inappropriate or just a bad idea.

? Do you know anyone who doesn't like to receive gifts? How does that make the giver feel?

? How can what Christ did for you be considered a gift?

Christmas Vacation (Christmas)

Ghosts of Christmas past

The movie   Comedy, Rated PG-13

This year the Griswold Family Christmas *should* be one for the storybooks. The relatives are coming, the gifts are wrapped, and the perfect tree has been cut down and decorated. Clark Griswold (Chevy Chase) even has plans to surprise his wife Ellen (Beverly D'Angelo) and the kids by putting in a new swimming pool with the signing bonus he anticipates receiving before the holidays. And then it all goes wrong. The bonus doesn't come; Cousin Eddie (Randy Quaid) and his family show up (parking their rusted-out RV in the driveway); both sets of in-laws arrive, yet can't seem to get along with each other; the dog chases a squirrel into the Christmas tree; the cat explodes; and the SWAT team shows up to join the festivities.

This clip   (about 4 minutes)

▶ **Start** / 0:31:51 / Clark walks across boards in his attic.

■ **Stop** / 0:35:42 / Clark falls down through the attic access door.

While hunting for the Christmas gifts he stashed away in the attic, Clark finds himself locked in and abandoned when Ellen takes her parents (E.G. Marshall and Doris Roberts) and her in-laws (John Randolph and Diane Ladd) shopping. As Clark digs through a wardrobe trunk to find something to keep him warm, he comes across a box of old home movies. Watching the holiday scenes from his childhood flicker across the screen, Clark is swept up in nostalgia and emotion.

By the Book

Deuteronomy 32:7; Proverbs 17:6; Ecclesiastes 11:8-10; Hebrews 10:25, 13:7

Where to take it

(?) What are some of your greatest memories of Christmas?

(?) What is your favorite Christmas ornament and why?

(?) How seriously does your family take their Christmas decorating?

(?) How important is the classic Christmas dinner to your family?

(?) If you were to find some of your old home movies, what would be revealed?

(?) Whom would you see in those videos who are no longer with you today?

(?) How do you feel when you think about those people?

A Cinderella Story

What controls your
perspective on life?

The movie   Comedy/Romance, Rated PG

In this modern twist on the classic fairy tale, Sam Montgomery (Hilary Duff) spends her days at a diner taking orders from her stepmother Fiona (Jennifer Coolidge) and her nights studying with hopes of attending Princeton. The one bright spot in Sam's life comes when she finds her Prince Charming online. When his identity is finally unveiled at a school dance, Sam is shocked to discover that her cyberspace prince is really Austin Ames (Chad Michael Murray), the star quarterback at her high school.

This clip (5 1/2 minutes)

▶ **Start** / 1:16:00 / Sam scrubs the diner floor.

■ **Stop** / 1:21:30 / Sam leaves the locker room.

Sam's dreams of attending Princeton and meeting her "prince" have been dashed. It seems she is destined to be Diner Girl forever. Life looks bleak, but her friends show her there is still hope. With her newfound perspective, she stands up to the stepmother who has controlled her life and then musters the courage to confront Austin in the locker room before the big football game.

By the Book

1 Samuel 16:7; Matthew 5:11, 5:43-44, 6:26; Luke 6:22; Hebrews 12:28

Where to take it

- Why does Sam seem so hopeless? What changes her perspective?

- Does having a purpose in life affect your perspective? What factors influence your perspective?

- Do you find it easy or difficult to count the blessings in your life? Explain.

- Sam found a "family" in an unlikely place. Have you experienced a family outside of your home? What did that experience mean to you?

- Describe a time when you experienced rejection.

- Have you ever experienced rejection because of your faith? How did you respond?

- What do you think about Sam's response to Austin?

- What should be the basis of our self-worth?

57

Confessions of a Teenage Drama Queen

Trailer

What if past lies came
back to haunt you?

The movie   Comedy, Rated PG

Lola (Lindsay Lohan) is forced to leave her home in New York City and move
to a New Jersey suburb. Desperate to fit in, she takes her skills as a "drama
queen" to the next level and begins to lie about her family and her past. Carla
Santini (Megan Fox) was the most popular girl in school before Lola showed
up, and she is determined to keep it that way. A war for popularity ensues with
lots of drama along the way.

This clip   (just over 4 minutes)

▶ **Start** / 1:05:36 / Lola enters the classroom, eager to
gloat about her trip to the party.

■ **Stop** / 1:09:50 / "Have you finally had enough?"

Feeling elated after attending a party with her idol, rock singer Stu Wolff
(Adam Garcia), Lola can't wait to share her experience with everyone at school.
Carla saw Lola at the party, but she is fearful of how this latest turn of events
will affect her own popularity. So she seizes the opportunity to expose Lola's
previous lies, and Lola is devastated to realize no one believes her.

By the Book

Psalm 59:12; Proverbs 6:16, 19; 19:5; Matthew 5:11; John 4:24, 5:41, 12:43

Where to take it

- Is there a difference between lying and dramatization?

- Why do you think lies have that snowball effect?

- Have you ever been in a situation where you exaggerated the truth just to fit in? Did people accept you more because of the lie? What happens when your lie is revealed?

- Do you think Jesus understands the battle for acceptance? Explain.

- What role do you think emotions play in a person's behavior?

- What should guide our behavior and our choices?

- How can a lie affect our relationship with God? How can it affect our relationship with others?

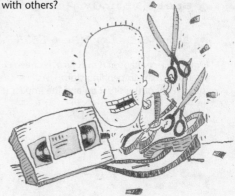

What if you knew the end of the world was coming?

The movie   Action/Drama, Rated PG-13

Global warming reaches disastrous proportions, which results in the Northern Hemisphere getting hit by a barrage of hurricanes, tornadoes, tidal waves, floods, and the dawning of a new Ice Age. Paleoclimatologist Jack Hall (Dennis Quaid) begins a relentless effort to track the storm's path and to save his son, Sam (Jake Gyllenhaal), who is stranded in the New York City Library.

This clip   (just over 2 minutes)

▶ **Start** / 0:51:46 / "Professor, I've got Jack Hall on the line."

■ **Stop** / 0:54:00 / "Save as many as you can."

Professor Terry Rapson (Ian Holm) has been collaborating with Jack to chart the direction of the impending storms. As Jack shares his projections, Terry realizes the severity of the situation and the impact it will have on his own life.

By the Book

Genesis 6:13, 9:11; Psalm 69:14, 121:7; Matthew 28:19; 1 Peter 4:7;
Revelation 21:4

Where to take it

(?) Have you experienced a natural disaster? What do you remember about the experience?

(?) Do you think natural disasters stem from the wrath of God?

(?) How has sin affected our environment?

(?) What responsibility do we have to protect our environment?

(?) What similarities do you see between the movie and the end times that are prophesied in the Bible?

(?) What emotions do you feel when you think about the end times?

(?) When do you think the prophecy regarding the end times will be fulfilled?

(?) How should we live our lives in light of the end-times prophecies?

(?) Do you think it is your responsibility to "save as many you can"? Why or why not?

Elf

(Father's Day)

Who's your daddy?

The movie Comedy, Rated PG

When Buddy (Will Farrell) was just a toddler in an orphanage, he snuck into Santa's (Ed Asner) toy bag and ended up at the North Pole. Having a warm spot in his heart for kids, Santa allows Papa Elf (Bob Newhart) to keep Buddy and raise him at his workshop among the other elves. When Buddy discovers he is really a human and not an elf, he sets off to New York City in search of his real father and his own identity.

This clip (about 4 1/2 minutes)

► **Start** / 0:45:18 / "Dad? Dad?"

■ **Stop** / 0:49:49 / Buddy stuffs his face with spaghetti laced with sugar.

Decked out in his yellow tights and pointy elf hat, Buddy sticks out like a sore thumb in New York City. When Buddy finally meets his biological father, Walter (James Caan) doesn't warm to the idea of having a full-grown son who thinks he's really an elf. Buddy eventually ends up at Walter's house with his wife, Emily (Mary Steenburgen), and their son, Michael (Daniel Tay). Buddy tries endlessly to win his father's affections, but Walter can barely tolerate Buddy.

**dads, heavenly father,
family relationships,
pleasing others, love,
expectations, hope**

By the Book

Psalm 127:3; Proverbs 23:24; Malachi 4:6; Luke 11:9-13; 2 Corinthians 5:8-9, 6:18; Ephesians 6:4; 1 John 3:1

Where to take it

? What type of relationship do you have with your father? What about your heavenly Father?

? Do you find yourself trying to please your dad the way Buddy does in this clip?

? Why is the love and approval of our fathers so important to us?

? What expectations do you put on your dad? Do you end up feeling let down or built up?

? Read Luke 11:9-13; 2 Corinthians 6:18; and 1 John 3:1. What does the Bible have to say about God being our Father?

? What are the attributes of a great father? How is God the model for our earthly fathers?

? How has your relationship with your earthly father affected the way you view God? How do you think God sees you as his child?

? What kind of parent do you want to be?

Envy

The movie Comedy, Rated PG-13

When Nick Vanderpark (Jack Black) hits the jackpot with his invention of "Vapoorize," his best friend Tim Dingman (Ben Stiller) is consumed by jealousy. Though Tim tries to convince Nick that a product designed to make fecal matter disappear is a ridiculous idea, the invention is a hit, and Nick's lifestyle undergoes a radical change. As Nick begins to gather all the amenities that come with wealth and power, Tim's envy builds, and he spends his days trying harder and harder to hold it in. When he realizes how deeply his jealousy has affected him, Tim goes on a journey to regain his sanity and recover his identity.

This clip (about 6 1/2 minutes)

▶ **Start** / 1:23:35 / "Hey."

■ **Stop** / 1:29:05 / "C'est la vie, as the Romans say."

After accidentally killing Nick's horse, Corky, Tim finds himself full of guilt as well as jealousy. Though his raging envy over Nick's new wealth causes Tim to keep the accident a secret at first, Tim realizes he is being eaten alive and needs to come clean. Tim confesses to Nick just how deep his bitterness and envy has become and what it was like to live in the shadows of a man who followed his dreams and became rich. Nick forgives Tim for the accident, offers to make Tim a partner in his business, and assures Tim that they are still best friends.

**coveting, lifestyle, jealousy, envy,
desires, bitterness, comparison**

By the Book

Exodus 20:17; 2 Samuel 11; Job 5:2; Psalm 32:5; Mark 7:20-23; James 3:14-16, 5:16; 1 Peter 2:1-3

Where to take it

- In your heart of hearts, are you a person who considers nice, expensive things to be really important? How much time and energy do you spend acquiring "stuff"?

- What is the difference between jealousy and envy?

- In this scene Tim tells Nick, "It's just another thing of yours that makes me miserable." Is there anyone you know whose things and possessions make you feel envious? In what ways?

- Some compare envy to a cancer that spreads throughout your whole being. In what ways is this correlation true?

- 2 Samuel 11 tells the story of what happened when King David allowed himself to be overcome by envy and covetousness. What were the consequences of his actions? What is the most surprising thing to you about this story?

- What are the benefits of confessing to a friend when there is something wrong between you—the way Tim finally does with Nick? Why do we sometimes keep ourselves from confessing bitterness or jealousy?

- Who suffers the most when you allow bitterness to take over your life? What can you do to remain free from envy and jealousy?

The Family Man

(Valentine's Day)

"I choose us"

The movie Comedy/Drama, Rated PG-13

Standing at an airport gate, Jack Campbell (Nicolas Cage) promises the girl of his dreams, Kate Reynolds (Téa Leoni), that he will come back for her when he finishes a one-year internship in London. Flash forward 13 years and Jack is now a single, hard-driving and very successful Wall Street trader. On Christmas Eve, Jack meets a mysterious stranger, Cash (Don Cheadle), who tells him he will be given a glimpse of a life he could have chosen. Jack awakens on Christmas morning and finds himself in bed with Kate—in their four-bedroom house in New Jersey. Jack's world is completely shaken up; his car is now a minivan, instead of a Ferrari, and his big-city career and upscale penthouse have been exchanged for a job at his father-in-law's tire store and a house full of family. As Jack's memories of his other life mix with his experiences in this new world, he begins to question the path he chose.

This clip (about 4 1/2 minutes)

▶ **Start** / 1:54:50 / Jack Campbell runs through the corridor of an airport.

⬛ **Stop** / 1:59:24 / "Okay." Scene fades to black.

After Jack receives a glimpse of what his life could have been like with Kate, Cash shows up again to tell him it's time to return to his old existence. That night, Jack falls asleep in a chair as he watches Kate sleep, and he awakens in his New York City apartment as if no time had passed. Jack knows he's changed, and he knows he wants the life he could have had with Kate. Jack tracks her down and finds her preparing to take a promotion in France. Like Jack, Kate has become a career-driven person who has forgotten about the life she wanted with Jack 13 years ago. Jack must decide if he should let Kate go or try to stop her before she walks onto the plane and out of his life again.

66

By the Book

Genesis 2:18, 2:24; Psalm 90:12; Proverbs 3:13-15; 1 Corinthians 13:4-7

Where to take it

- In your opinion, what is the definition of a "healthy" marriage?

- How do or how did you picture your marriage?

- What does the word love mean to you?

- What kind of an example of marriage did your parents show you?

- Who has a special marriage that you would like to copy?

- What does it mean to choose someone?

- Jack tells Kate, "You are a better person than I am, which made me a better person to be around you." How do you do that for the people you love?

The
Family Man

What world do you want—
career or family?

The movie Comedy/Drama, Rated PG-13

Standing at an airport gate, Jack Campbell (Nicolas Cage) promises the girl of
his dreams, Kate Reynolds (Téa Leoni), that he will come back for her when
he finishes a one-year internship in London. Flash forward 13 years and Jack is
now a single, hard-driving and very successful Wall Street trader. On Christmas
Eve, Jack meets a mysterious stranger, Cash (Don Cheadle), who tells him
he will be given a glimpse of a life he could have chosen. Jack awakens on
Christmas morning and finds himself in bed with Kate—in their four-bedroom
house in New Jersey. Jack's world is completely shaken up; his car is now a
minivan, instead of a Ferrari, and his big-city career and upscale penthouse
have been exchanged for a job at his father-in-law's tire store and a house full
of family. As Jack's memories of his other life mix with his experiences in this
new world, he begins to question the path he chose.

This clip (about 2 1/2 minutes)

▶ **Start** / 1:34:22 / Jack takes a book off the shelf.

■ **Stop** / 1:37:00 / Jack rests his head on the back
of the chair.

Believing he can combine the standard of living he had (before the glimpse)
with the family he didn't choose but has come to love, Jack finds a way to get
hired back with his old company in New York City. He tries to convince Kate
that this is the lifestyle they deserve. But Kate tells Jack that the life they built
together is the one she's always wanted.

By the Book

Ecclesiastes 6:12; Matthew 6:33; Philippians 2:3; Hebrews 13:5; James 4:14

Where to take it

(?) As you look into the future, what do you think it will take for you to consider yourself happy?

(?) What's more important to you—the relationships you will have, or the stuff you will own?

(?) Kate Campbell describes all her dreams for her family with Jack. She is willing to sacrifice it all for love. Are you or would you be willing to sacrifice everything for someone you love?

(?) What values does your family share?

(?) What do you want for your future family?

(?) Have you or a family member ever had to make a decision between a career move and family? If so, describe the struggle that took place before a decision was made.

69

Finding Nemo
(Father's Day)

Trailer

Has rebellion led you into trouble?

The movie — Animation/Comedy, Rated G

When Marlin (voiced by Albert Brooks) loses his wife and their brood of eggs to a nasty barracuda, he moves his one surviving son, Nemo (voiced by Alexander Gould), to the safest environment he can find. Marlin tries to be a good father to Nemo, but he is constantly worrying about what might happen to his little boy. When a diver snatches Nemo, Marlin is left with only one option: to find his son regardless of the dangers he may encounter.

This clip (about 7 minutes)

▶ **Start** / 0:08:39 / "Dad, can I go play, too? Can I?"

■ **Stop** / 0:15:15 / The boat's propeller knocks Marlin back as he says, "Nemo! No! Nemo!"

Marlin reluctantly agrees to allow Nemo to go to school. When he discovers that the teacher, Mr. Ray (voiced by Bob Peterson), is taking the kids to the edge of the reef, Marlin swims after them so he can bring Nemo home. Angry that his father is so overprotective, Nemo swims away from the security of the reef and encounters more than just a boat.

By the Book

Exodus 20:12; Proverbs 16:18; Romans 13:2; 1 Corinthians 10:23-24; Ephesians 6:1, 6:4

Where to take it

? In what ways do you feel your parents don't understand you?

? In what ways do you see your parents being fearful of what might happen to you?

? Have you ever rebelled against your parents' rules and wishes? What happened?

? Which of your parents' rules do you find unreasonable? Why?

? Why do we want freedom from our parents?

? What kind of communication is established between you and your parents? How could it be improved?

? What things do you intend to do differently when you have children of your own?

Flight of the Phoenix

Trailer

Where do you find your purpose?

The movie Action/Adventure, Rated PG-13

A group of misfits must fend for themselves after surviving the crash of their cargo plane in the Mongolian Desert. Led by pilot Frank Towns (Dennis Quaid), the men are forced to overcome adverse conditions in the sand, limited food and water, and the threat of desert smugglers in their quest to survive. When it becomes apparent that they will have to rescue themselves, Towns must pull the survivors together to dismantle the wrecked cargo plane and build a new one that will fly them to safety.

This clip (about 2 minutes)

▶ **Start** / 0:43:25 / "Do you think they are ever going to find us?"

⏹ **Stop** / 0:45:07 / "There are people counting on me."

James Liddle (Scott Michael Campbell), one of the crash survivors, takes off into the desert to try to find a way home. Knowing Liddle doesn't stand a chance against the dangers of the desert, Towns goes after him. Though Towns does his best to convince Liddle to return to the camp and survive there for as long as possible, Liddle doesn't see a reason why he should go back to a hopeless situation. But believing that rebuilding the plane is their only chance for survival, Liddle ends up convincing Towns that the crazy plan is worth a try.

goals, purpose, destiny,
perseverance,
determination,
love, hope

By the Book

Ecclesiastes 3:1-10; Romans 5:3-5, 8:24-25; 1 Corinthians 13:13; 2 Timothy
1:8-9; Hebrews 11:1

Where to take it

● Why do people hold on to hopes and dreams that may never come true?

● James says a person needs someone to *love*; if they cannot have that,
give them something to *hope* for; and if not that, something to *do*. What
about this statement makes sense to you?

● In your estimation, are hope and faith attributes that separate the weak
from the strong? Explain your answer.

● How is the soul connected to purpose and the way we live out our lives?

● How does one find purpose? How does purpose relate to our natural
abilities and experiences?

● 1 Corinthians 13:13 talks about faith, hope, and love. Which of these
areas are lacking in your day-to-day existence?

● What do you do to survive when a situation seems hopeless?

Freaky Friday

(Mother's Day)

Is there someone who really
understands you?

The movie Comedy/Drama, Rated PG-13

Anna Coleman (Lindsay Lohan) is a teenaged girl facing all the struggles that
high school brings. She argues incessantly with her mother, Tess (Jamie Lee
Curtis), and the two have a difficult time finding common ground. With a
little help from some special fortune cookies, the mother and daughter switch
bodies and discover what it's like to live in the other person's skin.

This clip (about 3 1/2 minutes)

▶ **Start** / 0:14:07 / Tess answers the phone.

■ **Stop** / 0:17:40 / Anna storms upstairs

After Tess finds out that Anna was sent to detention, she removes the door—
and subsequently all privacy—from Anna's bedroom. When Anna walks in and
discovers that her little brother has raided her room, she storms downstairs to
confront her mother. The conversation that follows leaves both Tess and Anna
frustrated and angry.

By the Book

Exodus 20:12; Psalm 37:8, 139:14-16; 1 Corinthians 13:4-7; Ephesians 4:26, 6:2; Colossians 3:21

Where to take it

(?) Why do you think parents and teens often argue?

(?) What makes you angry? How do you respond when you're angry?

(?) Do you feel like your parents really listen to you? Explain.

(?) Why do you think teenagers seek out people to confide in other than their parents?

(?) Is there someone in your life who really understands you?

(?) Do you feel God is the one who knows you best? If yes, how did you get to that point in your relationship with him? If not, what is hindering that relationship?

(?) What could you do to improve the relationship you have with your parents?

Friday Night Lights

Trailer
The power of friendship

The movie — Drama, Rated PG-13

In Odessa, Texas, nothing is more important than high school football, and nothing is more precious than a state championship ring. At the start of the 1988 season, the hopes and dreams of an entire town—players, parents, alumni, and supporters—rest on the shoulders of football coach Gary Gaines (Billy Bob Thornton). Always aware that the townspeople's opinions of him ride on the Panthers' latest performance, Gaines holds himself and his team together through insults and praise, heartache and triumph, sacrifice and glory.

This clip (about 3 minutes)

▶ **Start** / 1:29:00 / Scene starts with the team joining hands as Coach Gaines enters locker room.

⏹ **Stop** / 1:32:08 / "AMEN!"

Facing defeat after battling their way to the state championship game, the Permian High Panthers gather in the locker room at halftime and nervously await Coach Gaines' tirade. But the months spent getting to know his players on a personal level have had a powerful effect on Gaines. He discovers that his priorities have shifted, and winning is no longer the ultimate goal. As he speaks to his players, some of them for the last time, Gaines takes the opportunity to tell them what's really important—the relationships they've built and the memories they've made.

By the Book

Proverbs 17:17, 18:24; Luke 11:1-4; Philippians 4:6; James 5:15

Where to take it

- Coach Gaines gives a great description of friendship. Do you have this type of trust with another person? If so, with whom, and why?

- What does it mean to have a full heart?

- When do you find yourself praying the most?

- Would you ever pray with another person?

- Read Philippians 4:6 and James 5:15. What does the Bible say about the power of prayer?

- Read the Lord's Prayer in Luke 11:2-4. In what areas do you need God's help the most?

- How can you lean on your friends for strength instead of pushing them away?

Hidalgo

Trailer

What has the power to engulf you?

The movie Action/Drama, Rated PG-13

Having never lost a long distance race, Pony Express courier Frank Hopkins (Viggo Mortensen) and his horse, Hidalgo, are dubbed the world's greatest endurance horse and rider. When the story of Hopkins and Hidalgo spreads beyond America, Sheikh Riyadh (Omar Sharif) is insulted by the claim that a mixed breed horse is superior to his purebred Arabian horses. He challenges the cowboy and his mustang to compete in a grueling 3,000-mile race across a deadly stretch of the Arabian Desert called The Ocean of Fire.

This clip (about 2 minutes)

▶ **Start** / 0:50:55 / "Easy boys, a long way to Damascus."

◼ **Stop** / 0:52:58 / Hopkins and Hidalgo ride off after they dump muddy water.

Even before the race begins, Hopkins and his horse struggle to overcome not only the conditions of the race but also the scorn and persecution of all those who are betting against them. Only a few days into their long journey, a water break turns into a race for their lives.

**bad habits, sin,
consequences,
sowing and reaping,
choices**

By the Book

Hosea 10:12; Romans 6:23, 12:21; Colossians 3:25; Hebrews 12:1

Where to take it

? How does the picture of the sandstorm rushing up to engulf everyone remind you of the way sin can overtake a person?

? Can you think of other pictures that illustrate the way sin works?

? How do you think habits begin?

? Do you have any bad habits? How long have you had your bad habit? Do you consider this habit sin?

? "Start a habit, reap an attitude; reap an attitude, live a lifestyle." How does this statement strike you?

? What are some of the consequences of sin? How can sin in one part of your life affect every area of your life?

? In the clip, what must Hopkins and Hidalgo do to escape the sandstorm? Do you think it's possible to escape from sin? How?

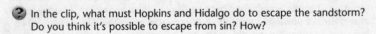

Home for the Holidays
(Thanksgiving)

Trailer

The good and bad of Mom and Dad

The movie Comedy/Drama, Rated PG-13

Claudia Larson (Holly Hunter) is making the trip home for Thanksgiving. Before she can even make it to the airport, she gets fired from her job, tries to kiss the boss who fired her, and finds out that her daughter is choosing to spend the holidays with her boyfriend instead of coming with her. Once she's at home, things rapidly progress from bad to worse as her various off-kilter family members gather for the Thanksgiving feast. Between the laughter, tears, and one airborne turkey, Claudia's bittersweet reunion with her dysfunctional family actually helps her find her way to a new beginning.

This clip (about 3 minutes)

▶ **Start** / 0:11:59 / The text MOM AND DAD appear.

⏹ **Stop** / 0:14:43 / Claudia looks up as cat spits out a dead mouse.

After a stressful flight, Claudia is greeted at the gate by her mom and dad, Adele (Anne Bancroft) and Henry Larson (Charles Durning). As her mother lectures her about her coat and her hair, Claudia finds herself immediately back in familiar yet unwanted territory: a grown woman treated like a child. While her father starts telling his old stories and her mother nags him about how he drives and where he parks, Claudia braces herself for a long weekend.

By the Book

Deuteronomy 5:16; Proverbs 10:1, 23:22; Malachi 4:6; Luke 11:13; Ephesians 6:4

Where to take it

(?) Describe Thanksgiving at your house.

(?) What are some of your favorite Thanksgiving traditions?

(?) How do your mom and dad make it special?

(?) What do you think your parents' childhoods were like?

(?) What values are you going to carry into your roles of mom and dad when you have children?

(?) What are you going to do differently from the way your parents did things? What will you do the same?

The Hours

Trailer

Do we always have a choice?

The movie Drama, Rated PG-13

Three women from three different generations struggle with depression and a sense of hopelessness. Virginia Woolf (Nicole Kidman) is an author fighting to overcome mental illness and thoughts of suicide in London in the 1920s. Laura Brown (Julianne Moore) is a depressed 1950s housewife who feels trapped by her life and responsibilities. Clarissa Vaughan (Meryl Streep) is a modern woman searching for meaning when she must face the death of her friend Richard (Ed Harris).

This clip (just over 6 minutes)

▶ **Start** / 1:40:15 / Clarissa answers the door.

■ **Stop** / 1:46:05 / "No one is going to forgive me."

Two of the women's lives collide when Clarissa invites Laura to Richard's funeral. Clarissa is struck by Laura's openness as she confesses why she abandoned her son 40 years earlier.

**regrets, taking responsibility,
consequences of sin,
forgiveness, suicide**

By the Book

Psalm 31:9-10, 14; 34:18; Matthew 6:14-15, 26:28; 2 Corinthians 7:10;
1 John 1:9

Where to take it

(?) Have you ever felt like you didn't belong? Explain.

(?) Why do you think people are so desperate to belong?

(?) What makes people contemplate something as desperate as suicide?

(?) How do you think God feels about suicide?

(?) What does it mean to regret? Is regret an appropriate response when we
make mistakes? Why, or why not?

(?) What would it be like to live a life without forgiveness?

(?) Where does forgiveness stem from?

(?) Laura said she chose life. What does "choosing life" mean to you? Do we
always have a choice?

**What are the origins of
your discontent?**

The movie Comedy, Rated PG

In the quaint little town of Whoville, everyone joyfully counts down the days, hours, and minutes until Christmas—everyone except the Grinch (Jim Carrey). He doesn't care for the people of Whoville or their Christmas festivities; such cheery celebrations turn his stomach. All the Whos in Whoville know about the Grinch but would like to forget about him—everyone except little Cindy Lou Who (Taylor Momsen). When Cindy Lou decides to make friends with the Grinch, she climbs up to his hideout in the mountain overlooking Whoville to convince him to join in the Christmas fun. What she doesn't know is that the Grinch already has his tiny heart set on making sure that Christmas doesn't come to Whoville at all.

This clip (about 6 1/2 minutes)

▶ **Start** / 0:26:24 / "He was a wonderful...whatever he was."

■ **Stop** / 0:32:56 / "Loathe entirely."

Cindy Lou interviews those who knew the Grinch when he was a boy growing up in Whoville. As each Who tells their version of the young Grinch, Cindy Lou discovers that even though a few Whos cared about the Grinch, many more ridiculed him and his efforts to fit in. Once Cindy Lou hears the whole story, she starts to understand how the Grinch came to live in the mountain overlooking Whoville and where his hatred of Christmas began.

By the Book

Job 36:13; Proverbs 10:12; Ecclesiastes 11:10; Ephesians 4:31; James 3:14-16

Where to take it

? Do you know of anyone who doesn't enjoy the holidays?

? Have you ever stopped to wonder why that person would rather be alone during a season when most people want to gather together?

? Why do you think some people look forward to the holidays all year long?

? Are your childhood memories of the holidays more positive or negative?

? What aspect of the holiday season brings tension to your home?

? What holiday traditions would you like to create when you have your own family and children?

? What can you do to make someone's holiday a bit brighter?

I, Robot

Trailer

Do you know the rules?

The movie Sci-Fi/Thriller, Rated PG-13

In a story inspired by the work of science fiction writer Isaac Asimov, Chicago Police Detective Del Spooner (Will Smith) reluctantly lives in a world where humans rely on robots as their personal assistants and helpmates. Del's bitterness toward the technology of the current year, 2035, stems from his memories of a late-night crash that sent him and an 11-year-old girl into an icy cold river. Del has never recovered from the fact that a robot rescued him instead of the young girl (based on its inhuman calculations of percentages and "survival of the fittest"). With his painful memories and prejudices working against him, Del must unravel a murder in which a robot is implicated, even though robots were supposedly programmed against committing such a crime.

This clip (about 1 minute)

▶ **Start** / 1:18:57 / Tablet reads: WHAT YOU SEE HERE. LAKE MICHIGAN.

■ **Stop** / 1:20:01 / "Program terminated."

Del embarks on a journey to discover why his programmer friend Dr. Alfred Lanning (James Cromwell) was murdered. As Del gathers information, he begins to wonder if the professor killed himself in an attempt to leave clues to the uprising of an evil robot empire. Del follows the bread crumbs his friend left behind—Hansel and Gretel-style—to help him stop the robots from taking over mankind. In a holographic conversation, Del is able to communicate with the deceased Lanning about the laws under which the robots were programmed and what they truly mean to the fate of mankind.

By the Book

Exodus 20:1-17; Deuteronomy 6:17, 11:1; Psalm 19:7-8, 111:7

Where to take it

- Do you know the "rules" according to the Bible? Where are they located?

- How many of the Ten Commandments can you recite off the top of your head? Look up Exodus 20:1-17 and see how many you knew, and how many you may have missed.

- How well do we stick to these Ten Commandments? What happens when the commandments are broken?

- Which commandments do you think are broken the most? Why?

- How do people sometimes justify breaking them, or just ignoring them?

- The professor says the three rules are perfect. What evidence do we have that the Ten Commandments are perfect?

- The clip states that the three laws would lead to a revolution. Throughout history, how have the Ten Commandments led to wars, revolutions, and protests?

- Which area of the Ten Commandments needs the most work in your life?

- Why do you think God gave us rules to live by?

What's a "normal" family?

The movie Animation/Comedy, Rated PG

In the golden age of superheroes, Mr. Incredible (voiced by Craig T. Nelson) is the master of bringing down the bad guys and rescuing the innocent. But when an overzealous fan interferes with a rescue, a superhero backlash begins, and people begin taking the heroes to court. In response, the federal government sends all superheroes and their families into protective relocation services to begin life again as "normal" people. But 15 years later, Mr. Incredible, who is now known by his secret identity— Bob Parr—desperately misses the good old days when he knew without a doubt who he was and what he was living for.

This clip (about 3 1/2 minutes)

▶ **Start** / 0:17:10 / Helen feeds Jack Jack at the dinner table.

■ **Stop** / 0:20:46 / "Lucky—uh, I meant about being normal."

The Parrs sit down for a nice family dinner, but there's a problem: they're all so focused on their own issues that no one is listening to anyone else. Violet's (voiced by Sarah Vowell) brain is totally occupied by a crush on a boy; Dash (voiced by Spencer Fox) is in trouble at school again; Jack Jack (voiced by Eli Fucile and Maeve Andrews) is happy just being a baby; and Bob feels his retirement from superhero work has taken away his significance. Meanwhile, Helen (voiced by Holly Hunter), who does everything within her human powers to create the ideal household for her husband and kids, realizes that her best efforts are not good enough as her family unit falls apart right before her eyes. Though everyone pretends to get along, the truth is that the Parr family is in chaos.

By the Book

Malachi 4:6; Ephesians 4:32, 6:1-4; Philippians 2:3, 4:8; 1 Timothy 3:4; Hebrews 10:24-25; James 3:14-16; 1 Peter 5:5

Where to take it

(?) How often does your family sit down to have dinner together? When it does, are they good times, or are they tense occasions?

(?) On average, how much time do you think your family spends together on a weekly basis? What do you enjoy about that family time?

(?) In this clip, we see the Incredibles trying to have a normal meal, but all of the family members seem to be off in their own worlds, with their own problems. How true is this with your family?

(?) If you could change one thing about the dynamic of your home, what would it be? Read Malachi 4:6; Ephesians 4:32; Ephesians 6:1-4; and 1 Timothy 3:4. What does Scripture have to say about family?

(?) How could you engage more with your family? With which person in your family do you have the hardest time getting along?

(?) The Parr children want to be normal and not have powers—especially if they're not allowed to use them very often. Describe what a "normal" household looks like.

(?) When the doorbell rings, the Incredibles sit back down at the table and pretend all is well. What secrets does your family keep from the rest of the world? How do these secrets affect the relationships within your home?

Jingle All the Way
(Christmas)

Trailer

Where's your Christmas spirit?

The movie   Action/Comedy, Rated PG-13

It's Christmas time, but Howard Langston (Arnold Schwarzenegger) hasn't caught the holiday spirit yet. Instead, he's become caught up in a quest to get his son, Jamie (Jake Lloyd), the gift he wants most: a Turbo Man action figure. Instead of thinking ahead and buying the gift in advance, Howard has waited until the very last minute—Christmas Eve. As he goes out in search of the toy, Howard quickly discovers that not only does every young boy in America want his own Turbo Man, but he also learns that their parents will do *anything* to get it.

This clip (about 6 minutes)

- ▶ **Start** / 0:42:15 / Howard Langston walks over to the counter at a coffee shop.

- ■ **Stop** / 0:48:05 / "I've already got the right answer. I win—ha, ha, ha."

Howard sets out for the journey of his life on Christmas Eve. He is convinced that if he can find this one toy for Jamie, the gift will make up for the many hours he's been away working. As Howard makes his way among the throngs who are also looking for Turbo Man, he has numerous run-ins with other equally desperate parents, including a mailman named Myron (Sinbad) bent on finding the same action figure for his boy. After searching the city for the better part of the day, Myron and Howard discuss the potential damage to their sons if they *don't* buy a Turbo Man. When they hear an offer over the radio that just may save the day, their conversation is over and the race is back on.

By the Book

Psalm 127:3; Proverbs 29:15; Luke 11:13, 12:34; Philippians 2:3; James 3:14-16

Where to take it

? How have you sometimes missed the mark when it comes to the true meaning of Christmas?

? Describe a holiday season when you (or your family) were more caught up in giving and receiving gifts than in celebrating the Savior's birth.

? Have you ever witnessed a scene like this first-hand, in which adults were behaving like children while trying to buy a certain gift? How did that make you feel about the Christmas season?

? What is the best Christmas gift you ever received? Why was it so special to you?

? What is the best Christmas gift you ever gave?

? We hear Myron talk about how his dad let him down one Christmas, yet he still remembers it as an adult. Did you ever feel as though your parents let you down over a gift?

? What is the most meaningful family Christmas celebration you can remember? What made it meaningful?

The Joy Luck Club
(Mother's Day)

Trailer

What makes us the people we are?

The movie Drama, Rated R

In an attempt to survive their perilous existence in war-torn China, four women form a gathering called the Joy Luck Club, and lifelong friendships are forged. Many years and many hardships later, the women have all immigrated to America and are struggling to raise their families amid the confusion of vastly differing cultures. Though each of the women wants the best for her American-born children, especially her daughters, difficulty communicating and unmet expectations sometimes cause heartache for the four families whose lives are deeply intertwined.

This clip (about 6 1/2 minutes)

▶ **Start** / 0:34:50 / "My mother always does this."

■ **Stop** / 0:41:29 / "I did it to myself."

In frustration over her mother's constant disapproval, Waverley Jong (Tamlyn Tomita) recalls her childhood mastery at chess and the pride and joy it brought her mother Lindo (Tsai Chin.) As she sifts back through her memories, Waverley begins to realize that the same approval she now longs to receive from her mother was the very reason that Waverley turned her back on the one thing that made her special.

By the Book

Exodus 20:12; 1 Samuel 2:3; Proverbs 11:2; Ezekiel 16:44; 2 Corinthians 10:17; 1 Timothy 4:12

Where to take it

? How does the parent-child relationship shape us into the people we become?

? What kinds of events or circumstances shaped your parents' personalities? How does that affect the way they treat you?

? Have you ever felt supported and encouraged by your parents? Do they show it when they're proud of you? Have you ever been embarrassed by their pride?

? Why do we sometimes feel as though pleasing Mom and Dad is just impossible to do?

? How important is your mom's and your dad's approval to you? How far would you go to gain that approval?

? When something goes wrong between you and your parents, are you willing and able to admit your mistakes? Who usually makes the first move to heal the broken relationship?

? What could you do to improve the level of communication with your parents?

King Arthur

Trailer

What are you fighting for?

The movie   Action/Adventure, Rated PG-13

Re-imagining one of history's most cherished heroes, director Antoine Fuqua portrays King Arthur as less of a legend and more of a man. During Rome's occupation of Britain, young boys are forced to serve in the Roman army for 15 years before earning the right to return to their homes as free men. A brotherhood of soldiers, Arthur (Clive Owen) and his Knights of the Round Table, is nearing the end of their service when they are sent on one last mission—escorting a Roman family to safety ahead of the Saxon army that is brutally invading Britain. Faced with a terrible decision, Arthur and his knights must decide if they will take the freedom they've earned or protect the country they love.

This clip   (about 2 minutes)

- ▶ **Start** / 1:29:32 / The doors of Hadrian's Wall swing open.
- ■ **Stop** / 1:31:42 / "Finally. A man worth killing."

Though each of his knights has chosen to leave rather than face certain death at the hands of the Saxons, Arthur prepares to make his own stand against the vast, dangerous army that is camped on the other side of Hadrian's Wall. On the eve of what will probably be his last battle, Arthur meets with Cerdic (Stellan Skarsgård), the leader of the Saxons, revealing the true reason each man has chosen to fight.

By the Book

2 Chronicles 15:7; Isaiah 1:17; John 16:33; 2 Corinthians 4:8-9;
2 Timothy 4:7

Where to take it

(?) What stirs your heart and makes you want to get involved?

(?) When have you stepped in to defend someone who could not defend himself or herself?

(?) How have your actions defined other people's opinions of you?

(?) How important is it to you to be known as a person of honor? What could you do to develop such a reputation?

(?) When in your life have you taken an unpopular stand and backed it up? What caused you to go against the crowd?

(?) How does it feel when you realize you are alone in your convictions or beliefs?

(?) What have you done to take up a cause and make a difference in the world?

(?) What is your first reaction to a situation that seems impossible to overcome?

(?) When have you succeeded against seemingly insurmountable odds? Why do you think you were able to succeed?

(?) What do you do when doubts arise? What can you do to stay strong?

Life as a House

The movie Drama, Rated R

George Monroe (Kevin Kline) is a middle-aged man who is alienated from those he loves most, especially his troubled teenaged son, Sam (Hayden Christensen). When George discovers he only has a short time left to live, he strives to reinvent his life. George invites his son to move in with him for the summer, hoping Sam will work with him to build his dream home. While working on the massive project, the father and son put together more than a home—they rebuild their relationship.

This clip (just under 5 minutes)

▶ **Start** / 0:17:38 / George collapses in front of his office building.

■ **Stop** / 0:22:30 / "I'm scared."

George has just been fired from his job of 20 years. As he leaves the office building, he collapses. When he wakes up in the hospital, George realizes the severity of his condition. Through a conversation with his nurse, he searches for purpose in the time he has left.

By the Book

Ecclesiastes 3:1-10; Malachi 4:6; Romans 14:8; James 4:14; Revelation 21:41

Where to take it

❓ Does the thought of death scare you? Why, or why not?

❓ Do you think it would be a blessing or a curse to know how much time you have left?

❓ If you knew when you were going to die, would it affect the way you live your life? What would you change?

❓ What do you perceive to be your purpose in life?

❓ What part do you think faith plays in discovering your purpose?

❓ How does the nurse help George during this difficult time? How can we help others when they are struggling?

❓ How can we make the most of the time we have?

The Lord of the Rings: The Two Towers

Is your mind overthrown?

The movie Fantasy/Adventure, Rated PG-13

With The Fellowship of the Ring broken, Frodo Baggins (Elijah Wood) and his ever-faithful friend Samwise Gamgee (Sean Astin) continue their journey to Mordor so they can destroy The One Ring in the fires of Mount Doom. If they are to find the way to their destination, they must trust Smeagol (Andy Serkis), the original owner of the Ring, to lead them. Meanwhile, the Dark Lord Sauron and evil sorcerer Saruman (Christopher Lee) have started to assemble an army of evil for an assault on the free kingdoms of Middle-earth—the War of the Ring has begun.

This clip (about 5 minutes)

▶ **Start** / 0:58:11 / "My lord, Gandalf the Grey is coming."

■ **Stop** / 1:03:33 / "Enough blood has been spilt on his account."

Aragorn (Viggo Mortensen), Legolas (Orlando Bloom), and Gimli (John Rhys-Davies) meet up with Gandalf (Sir Ian McKellen), who is back from the abyss. They go to see Theoden (Bernard Hill), King of Rohan, who has been put under a spell by Gríma Wormtongue (Brad Dourif) and the evil Saruman (Christopher Lee). The power of the spell has completely transformed Theoden and all but taken away his will to live. Gandalf draws the evil spirit out and restores the king to health.

By the Book

Romans 6:14, 6:22, 8:2; Titus 3:3; Hebrews 4:12, 12:1; 2 Peter 2:19

Where to take it

(?) Theoden is under such a spell that even his appearance has changed. What spells can people find themselves under? How do they change?

(?) Have you ever allowed someone to have too much influence over your life? Describe what happened.

(?) Describe a time when you had something in your life that took the place of God. What did it change about you?

(?) What did it take for you to realize that your priorities were dangerously out of line?

(?) Gandalf tells Theoden, "Your fingers would remember their old strength better if they grasped your sword." How can this wisdom apply to the Bible?

(?) What metaphors are used to describe the Word of God?

(?) Describe a time when family members, friends, or even your church helped you when you felt consumed by a certain sin. How did you feel before and after they helped you?

The Lord of the Rings: The Two Towers

Trailer

What is worth fighting for?

The movie Fantasy/Adventure, Rated PG-13

With The Fellowship of the Ring broken, Frodo Baggins (Elijah Wood) and his ever-faithful friend Samwise Gamgee (Sean Astin) continue their journey to Mordor so they can destroy The One Ring in the fires of Mount Doom. If they are to find the way to their destination, they must trust Smeagol (Andy Serkis), the original owner of the Ring, to lead them. Meanwhile, the Dark Lord Sauron and evil sorcerer Saruman (Christopher Lee) have started to assemble an army of evil for an assault on the free kingdoms of Middle-earth—the War of the Ring has begun.

This clip (about 5 minutes)

▶ **Start** / 2:43:43 / Frodo pulls a sword on Sam.

■ **Stop** / 2:49:00 / Sam says, "Samwise the Brave."

The longer Frodo is in possession of the Ring, the deeper he's pulled into the darkness of its power. In a moment of madness, Frodo attacks his friend Sam. As he comes back to himself and realizes what he almost did, Frodo becomes discouraged. Sam talks to Frodo about what he has come to understand about the struggle they are facing.

By the Book

Proverbs 18:24, 27:17; Ecclesiastes 4:9-10; John 15:13; Hebrews 11:32-40; James 1:2-3

Where to take it

? Describe your friendships. Do you have any relationships like Frodo's and Sam's—a friendship that would go with you anywhere? Share about a time when you and your friend conquered a dark time in your life.

? Proverbs 27:17 talks about iron sharpening iron, so one friend sharpens another. What do you think this means? How do you see this happening in your friendships?

? What are some ways you could be sharpening your friends? How do you need to be sharpened?

? Sam talks to Frodo about the great stories—the ones that really matter. Which Bible stories speak to you the most? How do they give you hope? What do they teach you?

? Sam says, "In the end, it is only a passing thing, this shadow." What does he mean? Compare what he says with what the Bible tells us about our time on earth.

? Sam tells Frodo that people in those great stories had lots of chances to turn back, but they kept going because they were holding onto something. Think about the times in your life when you turned back and the times when you kept going. What did you learn from those experiences?

? Talk about the things in your world that are worth fighting for.

The Lord of the Rings: The Two Towers

What voices control you?

The movie Fantasy/Adventure, Rated PG-13

With The Fellowship of the Ring broken, Frodo Baggins (Elijah Wood) and his ever-faithful friend Samwise Gamgee (Sean Astin) continue their journey to Mordor so they can destroy The One Ring in the fires of Mount Doom. If they are to find the way to their destination, they must trust Smeagol (Andy Serkis), the original owner of the Ring, to lead them. Meanwhile, the Dark Lord Sauron and evil sorcerer Saruman (Christopher Lee) have started to assemble an army of evil for an assault on the free kingdoms of Middle-earth—the War of the Ring has begun.

This clip (about 3 1/2 minutes)

▶ **Start** / 1:13:37 / "We wants it. We needs it."

■ **Stop** / 1:16:01 / "Smeagol is free!"

Frodo and Sam's guide, Smeagol, was the first to discover the Ring. And after many years its evil presence has split Smeagol into two warring personalities who torment the poor creature's soul. Most of the time, the bad side (Gollum) wins the battle. Gollum wants the ring. He hates the hobbits because he believes they stole it from him. But Smeagol (the good side) likes Frodo and wants to help him. Gollum reminds Smeagol of all the evil he has done, but Smeagol realizes things can be different now. For the first time, Smeagol feels released from the snare of Gollum's unbridled jealousy and greed for the Ring that has ruled their lives.

**distractions, temptations,
Satan, accusations, lies,
double-mindedness,
sin nature, greed**

By the Book

Proverbs 11:6; Matthew 26:41; Luke 12:15; Romans 7:14-25, 8:3;
1 Corinthians 10:13; James 4:7-8

Where to take it

(?) What do you struggle with when it comes to the gray areas of life?

(?) Do you ever have conversations with yourself in an
attempt to justify something you know is wrong?
Describe.

(?) Gollum tries to disrupt the good that Smeagol
wants to do. How do contrasting thoughts
play a part in your everyday decisions?

(?) James 4:7-8 says to resist the devil
and he will flee. What does it
mean to draw near to God?

(?) Smeagol tells Gollum that his
master (Frodo) will take care
of Smeagol now and Gollum
should just go away and never
come back. How can we call
God our Master and tell the
enemy (Satan) to leave?

(?) The Bible refers to Satan as the accuser
of our souls. How does Satan act like Gollum in your mind?
What do you need to remember in order to fight his lies?

(?) Describe a time in your life when you were at war with yourself over a
particular decision. Which side of you won?

Lost in Translation

Trailer

Ever feel like God is speaking a different language?

The movie — Drama, Rated R

Bob Harris (Bill Murray) is a washed-up American movie star who has come to Toyko to shoot a commercial for a well-known Japanese whiskey. Charlotte (Scarlett Johansson), who is also an American, is visiting Japan with John (Giovanni Ribisi), her photographer husband who is so caught up with his work that he has little time to spend with her. Unable to sleep, these two lonely souls meet at the hotel bar one night. And before long, a new friendship develops between them, helping Bob and Charlotte face their feelings of isolation not only in this unfamiliar culture, but also in their own lives.

This clip (just over 3 minutes)

▶ **Start** / 0:08:30 / Scene opens on the set of the commercial.

■ **Stop** / 0:11:56 / Japanese director exclaims, "Cut-o, cut-o, cut-o!"

Bob is on the set of the commercial shoot. As he waits for the interpreter (Akiko Takeshita) to explain the director's (Yutaka Tadokoro) lengthy instructions, Bob gets the feeling that quite a bit of information isn't surviving the translation. Bob attempts to follow the few cues that are given to him, but he can't seem to please the man in charge.

communication, Bible, frustration,
God's will, hearing God,
unconfessed sin, prayer

By the Book

2 Chronicles 7:14; Jeremiah 29:12-13; Matthew 6:5-6; Luke 11:1-4; John 8:43, 13:7; 1 Corinthians 14:33; Philippians 4:6

Where to take it

❓ What keeps you from talking to God?

❓ Why do we sometimes feel as though our prayers aren't making it past the ceiling?

❓ How and why does sin come between God and us?

❓ In this scene, Bob has trouble understanding what the director wants from him. Do you ever feel that your relationship with God is similar—that he is frustrated with you and unhappy with your performance?

❓ Does God judge us based on our actions? Do you think he is disappointed in you?

❓ Read Matthew 6:5-6 and Luke 11:1-4. What does the Bible say about prayer and how to do it?

❓ What can we do to make sure the lines of communication between God and us stay clear?

Luther

' Are you angry with God?

The movie Drama, Rated PG-13

Martin Luther (Joseph Fiennes) is a German monk who takes on the most powerful institution of his time: the Catholic Church. Tired of the church's many indiscretions, Luther chooses to follow God rather than the politics of the day. In an attempt to make a difference, Luther confronts the church, stating his case in his 95 Theses—which he boldly nails to the church door in Wittenburg.

This clip (about 2 minutes)

▶ **Start** / 0:05:50 / "Shut up, shut up! Leave me alone!"

■ **Stop** / 0:08:03 / "I am yours. Save me."

Abbot Johann von Staupitz (Bruno Ganz), the father of the monastery where Luther first lives, finds the young monk wrestling with what he believes about God's character. Luther feels unworthy to be a minister, so the older monk challenges Luther to be honest about his deeper fears and tells him that neither fighting with the devil nor blaming God will stop his pain. The elder monk shows Luther how to find peace for his troubled soul.

bitterness, anger, weaknesses, sanctification, turmoil, wrestling, Satan, confusion, doubt, unworthiness

By the Book

Deuteronomy 32:4; Matthew 16:23; Romans 7:14-25, 8:2, 16:20; Ephesians 6:12; 1 Peter 5:8

Where to take it

(?) How do we tend to beat ourselves up? In what ways do you put yourself down over your past mistakes?

(?) "The devil has had 5,000 years of practice; he knows all the weak spots." After hearing this line in the movie, does it give you a new perspective on Satan's ways? Read Romans 7:14-25 and Romans 8:2. What does the Bible say about being in bondage to our weak spots?

(?) Martin Luther considered himself too full of sin to be a priest. Do you feel this way when it comes to being a fully devoted follower of God?

(?) Read Deuteronomy 32:4. What does it mean to say that God is just?

(?) Name as many attributes of God as you can think of. Which ones do you wrestle with?

(?) The older monk tells Luther, "God isn't angry with you. You are angry with God." In what ways are you angry with God?

(?) "I am yours. Save me." What does this mean to you?

The Matrix Reloaded

Do you believe in purpose?

The movie Drama, Rated R

In the world where the machines use humans for fuel, Morpheus (Laurence Fishburne) and Trinity (Carrie-Anne Moss) believe Neo (Keanu Reeves) is The Chosen One who will defeat the machines. While more and more individuals are being freed from the Matrix, the machines are amassing an army of 250,000 robots to tunnel to Zion and destroy it. If successful, they win the war, and the human race is doomed forever.

This clip (under 1 minute)

▶ **Start** / 1:41:25 / "All of our lives we have fought this war. Tonight, I believe we can end it."

■ **Stop** / 1:42:12 / "I believe this night holds, for every one of us, the very meaning of our lives."

Morpheus and crew are on the verge of a clash with the machines. Morpheus tells his fellow warriors what he believes about the battle they are going to fight. He is confident there is nothing accidental about all they have done and all they are about to do.

By the Book

Esther 4:14, 7:1-10; Ecclesiastes 6:10, 9:2-3; Jeremiah 1:19; John 16:33; Colossians 1:6

Where to take it

? What does *chance* mean to you? Do you think our lives are subject to chance?

? What is *providence*? What is *destiny*? What do you believe about them?

? What do you think is the relationship between free will and providence?

? How do your dreams for your life and God's purpose for your life come into alignment? How do they conflict?

? How do you think God is going to use you to carry out your purpose?

? Have you ever met someone who was so compelling about his faith that it made you want to believe? Describe this person.

? Describe a time when you were faced with something so huge that you knew it was going to take all the faith, courage, and stamina you had.

? Read Esther 4:14 and Esther 7:1-10. How does this story demonstrate victory over incredible odds? What does it say about Queen Esther's courage?

Trailer
Where do you find significance?

The movie Comedy/Drama, Rated PG-13

Cady Heron (Lindsay Lohan) spent most of her life in the wilds of Africa with her zoologist parents. When her family returns to the United States, Cady discovers that the American high school is a jungle all its own. She soon finds herself in the middle of a conspiracy to bring down the "Plastics"—the mean-spirited girls who rule the school.

This clip (about 3 minutes)

▶ **Start** / 1:26:30 / Cady and the other Mathletes walk into the gymnasium.

⏹ **Stop** / 1:29:28 / "All right, have a good time everyone."

Cady and her Mathletes teammates arrive at the Spring Fling dance just as the king and queen are about to be announced. Much to her surprise, Cady is chosen to be queen. She makes her way onstage to accept the crown but realizes she has a much better idea for how to use this shiny piece of plastic.

By the Book

Proverbs 16:28, 20:3; Luke 12:6-7; Ephesians 4:25-27; Philippians 2:3

Where to take it

? How would you describe your friends?

? Are you part of the popular crowd at your school? Why do you think students strive so hard to be part of the elite group instead of being okay with the people they hang out with?

? What is the one thing you dislike most about the different cliques in your school?

? In this clip, what stuck out to you as an honest moment?

? Cady uses the platform of Spring Fling Queen to share the honor with different groups in her class. What are some ways you could do that at your school?

? Looking back, have you ever treated others disrespectfully just because they were different or didn't fit in? Have you ever been on the receiving end of this kind of treatment? Describe what happened.

? What have you learned from your experiences with cliques and friendship groups?

Miracle
(Independence Day)

Trailer
What "team" do you belong to?

The movie Drama, Rated PG

The year is 1980, and the winter Olympics are to be held in Lake Placid, New York. Since the Russian National Team has dominated the sport of hockey for the past 15 years, no one envisions that Team U.S.A. will have much success during the upcoming Games. But long-time collegiate coach Herb Brooks (Kurt Russell), who was chosen to lead the U.S. Olympic Team, believes he has the formula to win the gold medal. Brooks is confident the winning team won't consist of the most talented players on the ice; it will be those who possess the right amount of will and determination. Brooks' unorthodox coaching methods raise concerns with the committee who hired him, his own assistant coaches, and even the team members. But as he holds to what he believes, he pushes his team beyond what anyone ever thought possible.

This clip (about 8 minutes)

▶ **Start** / 0:38:49 / "Get a whistle."

■ **Stop** / 0:46:30 / "That's all, gentlemen."

After a disappointing performance against Norway, one thing is evident to Coach Brooks about his young squad: they are playing like individuals, not a team. Brooks calls everyone back to the ice for a post-game practice. Brooks wants to teach his team that the name on the front of the jerseys is more important than the names on the back. Through an unrelenting series of sprints, Brooks works the young men to their breaking points. Then he takes the opportunity to help his players realize who—and what—they are playing for.

By the Book

Psalm 31:24, 133:1; Romans 12:4-5; 1 Corinthians 12:20; Philippians 4:13; 1 Thessalonians 5:11; Hebrews 10:24; James 1:2-3

Where to take it

- Have you ever had to earn a place on a team? As a result, did it mean more to you?

- Do you see yourself as someone who would be willing to work as hard as these young men had to work to be part of a team?

- In James 1:2-3, what does the Bible have to say about endurance?

- What do you think is your spiritual breaking point? Have you ever been there? What happened on the other side?

- What does unity mean to you?

- Read Psalm 133:1. What does the Bible say about unity?

- Read Romans 12:5. What does the Bible say about the body of Christ?

My Big Fat Greek Wedding

Trailer

How much trouble would you go
through for someone you love?

The movie Comedy/Romance, Rated PG

Toula (Nia Vardalos) is unmarried, and her family won't let her forget it. Her
Greek culture teaches Greek girls that they have three purposes in life: to marry
a Greek man, to have Greek babies, and to feed everybody until death. While
the rest of her family has followed this custom, Toula is 30 years old and has
no real prospects for marriage, so she decides to make some changes in her
life. When she does find a man she loves, he is not Greek. Their love will not
only have to conquer all, but it will have to take on her very loving, very quirky,
and very Greek family.

This clip (4 minutes)

▶ **Start** / 0:48:28 / "Hi."

■ **Stop** / 0:52:28 / "Thank you so much...thank you."

Ian proposes to Toula, but her excitement is short-lived. Because Ian isn't
Greek, they cannot get married in her family's church. But Toula knows it
would mean a lot to her parents if they could, so she feels caught between
her family and the man she loves. She wants to run away from the stress and
just elope; but Ian won't let her. He tells her he won't let anything stand in
the way of their happiness together, so he agrees to be baptized in the Greek
Orthodox Church.

By the Book

Genesis 2:18, 2:24; Mark 1:4, 1:8; Romans 6:3; 1 Corinthians 7:16;
2 Corinthians 6:14; Ephesians 5:33; Philippians 2:3; 1 Peter 3:21

Where to take it

- Do you know any couples who don't share the same beliefs? How do they handle it?

- When you watch this scene and see what Ian does for Toula, do you find it noble or wrong?

- Would you be willing to change your denomination for your spouse? Why or why not?

- Would you even date someone who wasn't likeminded in your religion? What kinds of problems can be caused by that kind of relationship?

- Toula wonders if Ian will one day wake up and decide she isn't worth all the trouble of becoming part of the Greek Orthodox denomination. Why do you think she felt this way? Would you feel that way?

- In Mark 1:4 and 1:8, what does the Bible say about baptism?

- Read Romans 6:3 and 1 Peter 3:21. How does baptism symbolize an ongoing pursuit of God?

115

Every moment counts

The movie · Drama, Rated PG-13

Bob Jones (Michael Keaton) is a successful executive with a loving wife (Nicole Kidman) and a baby on the way. Diagnosed with terminal cancer and given only a few months to live, Bob decides to make a video diary of his life for his child, whom he may never see. What starts as a plan to allow someone else to know him results in Bob discovering a lot about his life and himself, not all of which makes him proud. With his time running out, he tries to make peace with his wife, with his family, and with himself. In the midst of it all, he learns the true meaning of life: the gift of love.

This clip (about 4 1/2 minutes)

▶ **Start** / 0:05:19 / "My name...I am Bob Jones."

◼ **Stop** / 0:09:50 / "I hate my own home movies. I always did."

Bob starts his first videotaped message to his unborn child. He hopes the video will capture the kind of man he was and what his life was like. Bob films himself looking through old photo albums and watching home movies as he tries to pass on some life lessons and family history to his child.

By the Book

Psalm 127:3, 139:14-16; Jeremiah 1:5; 1 Corinthians 13:13;
Ephesians 3:1-8, 6:4

Where to take it

(?) What do old family photos and home movies reveal about your family?

(?) If you could choose one word to describe your family, what would it be?

(?) If you knew your life was ending, would you want to put your life on film
for your loved ones to watch after you were gone? Why or why not?

(?) If you've lost someone you love, did that
person leave something for you? What
does it mean to you?

(?) When you get to the end of your life,
what kinds of things will be important
to you?

(?) If you were to make a video like Bob did,
what are some pieces of wisdom you've
learned during your lifetime that you'd
want to record?

(?) How do you want to be remembered by
those you leave behind?

My Life

Unanswered prayers

The movie Drama, Rated PG-13

Bob Jones (Michael Keaton) is a successful executive with a loving wife (Nicole Kidman) and a baby on the way. Diagnosed with terminal cancer and given only a few months to live, Bob decides to make a video diary of his life for his child, whom he may never see. What starts as a plan to allow someone else to know him results in Bob discovering a lot about his life and himself, not all of which makes him proud. With his time running out, he tries to make peace with his wife, with his family, and with himself. In the midst of it all, he learns the true meaning of life: the gift of love.

This clip (about 2 1/2 minutes)

▶ **Start** / 0:01:53 / "Star light, star bright..."

■ **Stop** / 0:04:22 / Bobbie shuts the closet door.

Young Bobbie Jones (Danny Rimmer) prays to God about something he wants more than anything in the world. He promises God he will tell everyone about the wonderful thing God did. Confident his prayer will be answered the next day, Bobbie invites everyone in the school over to his house. After Bobbie and the other kids race to his backyard, he discovers he didn't get what he asked for. Disappointed and embarrassed, Bobbie hides in his room, angry that God didn't answer his prayer.

By the Book

Psalm 66:20; Matthew 6:5-6, 7:7, 18:18-19, 21:22; Luke 11:1-4; Philippians 4:6; James 4:3; 1 Peter 1:3-8

Where to take it

Do you ever try to bargain with God the way Bobbie does in this clip? What promises have you made to him?

In Matthew 6:5-6 and Luke 11:1-4, what did Jesus teach about prayer?

What are the similarities between how Jesus prayed and how Bobbie prayed? What are the differences?

Bobbie had absolutely no doubt that his prayer would be answered. When is the last time you had such confidence?

When a prayer is answered the way you specifically asked, how does it build your faith?

Describe a time when you diligently and wholeheartedly prayed for something but it didn't happen.

When a prayer is not answered the way you specifically asked, how does it build your faith?

What are your top three prayer requests today?

Have your group listen to the Garth Brooks song, "Unanswered Prayers." Ask your group to share about the thoughts and emotions it evokes in them.

Trailer

Who do people say that you are?

The movie   Drama, Rated PG-13

Bob Jones (Michael Keaton) is a successful executive with a loving wife (Nicole Kidman) and a baby on the way. Diagnosed with terminal cancer and given only a few months to live, Bob decides to make a video diary of his life for his child, whom he may never see. What starts as a plan to allow someone else to know him results in Bob discovering a lot about his life and himself, not all of which makes him proud. With his time running out, he tries to make peace with his wife, with his family, and with himself. In the midst of it all, he learns the true meaning of life: the gift of love.

This clip   (about 3 1/2 minutes)

▶ **Start** / 0:13:14 / "George, come on in. Give me a minute, would you?"

■ **Stop** / 0:16:45 / Scene ends with Bob sitting by himself at a conference table.

Bob asks George (Rudi Davis), one of his employees, to videotape various people around the office so he can include their comments in his video diary. When Bob asks how the filming is going, George reluctantly shows him the footage he's recorded so far. Watching his coworkers search for something to say is a sobering moment for Bob.

By the Book

Proverbs 11:13, 22:1; Ecclesiastes 1:11, 7:1; Matthew 16:13-20

Where to take it

? What's the best thing anyone ever said about you?

? If someone were to interview the people you hang out with, what would they say about you?

? Do you think other people's perceptions of you are close to who you really are?

? How open are you with your friends, and how much do you reveal your true self?

? What would you want people to remember about you? What do you want them to say about you at your funeral?

? If you'd received the type of comments Bob's coworkers made about him, would it make you defensive, or would it be an agent of change in your life?

? Matthew 16:13-20 talks about an instance where Jesus asks his disciples what people were saying about him. What were people saying about Jesus? Why do you think Jesus asked this question?

Mystery Men
(Halloween)

What superhero were you for Halloween?

The movie   Action/Comedy, Rated PG-13

A trio of socially inept misfits has been trying to break into the superhero scene for years. Unfortunately, the true defender of Champion City, Captain Amazing (Greg Kinnear), has done such a wonderful job fighting villains that other superheroes are unnecessary. When Captain Amazing falls into the hands of the evil madman Casanova Frankenstein (Geoffrey Rush) and his disco-dancing henchmen, there's suddenly a chance for the wannabes to show what they can do.

This clip   (about 8 minutes)

▶ **Start** / 0:36:38 / "We're looking for the one they call The Invisible Boy."

■ **Stop** / 0:44:31 / "Like so many things we do."

After a failed attempt to rescue Captain Amazing, The Shoveller (William H. Macy), The Blue Raja (Hank Azaria), and their leader, Mr. Furious (Ben Stiller), agree they need to add some new talent to their roster. They find a young man (Kel Mitchell) who claims to have the power to make himself invisible. When the gang is regrettably unable to ditch the self-assured and super-flatulent The Spleen (Paul Reubens) and then realizes more reinforcements are still necessary, they decide to host tryouts for any other crime fighters who want to join their mission to foil Casanova's plans to destroy the city.

122

By the Book

1 Chronicles 29:12; Proverbs 25:14; Ecclesiastes 9:11; Luke 12:48b;
Romans 11:29, 15:1

Where to take it

? What are some of your most memorable Halloween costumes?

? As a child, who were your favorite superheroes?

? When you look at these grown-ups who want to be heroes, do you see it as a noble thing or a waste of time?

? What group are you a part of that might seem ridiculous or juvenile to others, but it means something to you?

? In this clip, we see people who want to use their unusual talents and powers to fight crime and make the world a better place. What unusual talents or gifts do you have that could benefit others?

? What talent(s) do you wish you had? What would you do with that talent?

? What does the Bible say in the above verses about gifts and talents and how we use them?

? What happens when people use their talents for the wrong reasons?

Napoleon Dynamite

Trailer

How far would you go for a friend?

The movie Comedy, Rated PG

Napoleon Dynamite (Jon Heder) is an awkward teenager living in a small town in Idaho with his grandma (Sandy Martin) and his chat-room-cruising older brother Kip (Aaron Ruell). Despite his outcast status at the high school, Napoleon finds a purpose when he decides to help his best friend, Pedro (Efren Ramirez), win the title of student body president.

This clip (about 5 minutes)

▶ **Start** / 1:18:36 / "I didn't want to be president anyway."

⏹ **Stop** / 1:23:15 / Scene ends with Pedro smiling.

Pedro enters the election for student body president; but at the last minute, he gets cold feet when he sees the speech and skit that Summer Wheatley (Haylie Duff), the current student body president, has prepared. Pedro was unaware that a skit was part of the election process, so he decides to throw in the towel without even promising the students to "make their wildest dreams come true." Though Pedro feels he's been beaten before he even goes on stage, Napoleon has a plan. In place of the skit, Napoleon—knowing he could face the laughter and further rejection of the entire school—does a dance that causes the student body to jump to their feet at the end of the song. Pedro realizes that because of what his friend has done for him, the title of student body president is a lock.

By the Book

1 Samuel 16:7; Proverbs 14:12, 17:17, 18:24, 20:6, 27:6; Ecclesiastes 4:9-10; John 15:13; Philippians 2:1-4

Where to take it

(?) What does the term "best friend" mean to you? How is a best friend different from a boyfriend or girlfriend or from a regular friend?

(?) What are the top five traits you desire in a friend? Which of these traits do you possess?

(?) Read John 15:13, Proverbs 27:6, and Proverbs 17:17. What does the Bible have to say about true friendship? What does it say about what a friend isn't?

(?) In order to help a friend, Napoleon takes a huge step out of his comfort zone. Would you have done the same? Why or why not?

(?) Napoleon also tells Pedro to "follow his heart." What does this phrase mean to you?

(?) Read Proverbs 14:12. Is there ever a time when following your heart is not a good idea?

(?) Describe a time you went out of your way to help a friend succeed in something he or she really wanted. What, if anything, did you gain from the experience? What did you learn about doing something entirely for the benefit of someone else?

(?) Have you ever let a friend down? Was there reconciliation? Is it possible to have a friendship with someone who doesn't treat you with respect?

Notting Hill
(Valentine's Day)

Trailer

Just a girl—standing in front of a
boy—asking him to love her

The movie Romantic Comedy, Rated PG-13

Beautiful American movie star Anna Scott (Julia Roberts) has little time for
relationships and absolutely no luck with love until she meets William Thacker
(Hugh Grant), a frumpy British bookstore owner. After a false start or two, this
unlikely pair begins dating in secret. But when the British press gets wind of
their romance, William and Anna discover just how different two worlds can
be.

This clip (about 3 minutes)

▶ **Start** / 1:44:18 / "Anna, look...um...I'm a fairly level-
headed bloke."

■ **Stop** / 1:46:54 / Anna Scott walks out of the
bookshop.

Before leaving town, Anna comes by William's bookstore to ask him an
important question: If she decided to stay, would there be any chance for
them to rekindle their relationship? William declines her offer, explaining
that their worlds are too different and that if she were to hurt him again, he
doesn't think he would recover. William believes that Anna could easily break
away from him, but because her photos and films are everywhere, he fears he
wouldn't be able to escape her. She tries to help him understand that her fame
doesn't shield her from hurt or rejection, nor does it take away her desire to
be loved by him.

By the Book

Proverbs 13:12, 20:6, 21:21; 1 Corinthians 13:4-7; Philippians 3:8; 1 John 4:18

Where to take it

What do you think true love really is?

In 1 Corinthians 13:4-7, how does the Bible define love?

In your opinion, what does the word rejection mean?

Have you ever offered your heart to another person, just to have it trampled on? How did that change the way you guard your heart?

What do you know about God that leads you to believe he cares about broken hearts and failed relationships?

Have you ever had to end a relationship with someone else? How did you go about it?

Have you ever turned down someone's love and affection for you because you were afraid of being hurt? Where do you think that fear came from?

The Passion of the Christ
(Good Friday and Easter)

The way we pray

The movie — Drama, Rated R

From his anguished prayer in the garden of Gethsemane to his final breath on the cross at Golgotha, this movie portrays what one might have witnessed while following Jesus Christ through the last 12 hours of his life on earth. Between the forces at war to destroy him and the devoted few who love him, Jesus (James Caviezel) takes his final steps down the road he came to walk—a road of suffering and sacrifice for all of mankind.

This clip (about 3 minutes)

▶ **Start** / 0:04:40 / Peter, James, and John look upon Jesus as he prays.

■ **Stop** / 0:07:30 / Jesus falls to the ground.

Jesus brings three of his disciples with him to the garden of Gethsemane so they can watch and pray; he knows the time has come for him to fulfill the purpose for which he was sent to earth. Jesus is visibly distraught—to the point of physical agony—as he prays and wrestles with the decision to follow his Father's will. As he cries out to God, another voice begins to speak to him. Satan (Rosalinda Celantano) tries to get Jesus to question what he has been asked to do.

By the Book

Matthew 26:36-46; Mark 8:33; Luke 22:39-46; Acts 2:22-24; Hebrews 2:9; 1 Peter 2:21-24

Where to take it

(?) What do you know about the garden of Gethsemane? Why do you think Jesus went there that night to pray?

(?) Why do you think Jesus took his closest friends with him?

(?) What did Jesus mean when he asked his Father to let the "chalice pass from me"?

(?) Jesus knew exactly what God's purpose for him was. Do you think he was trying to avoid the pain and suffering the crucifixion would bring?

(?) Which part of Jesus' prayer was the most significant to you? Which parts of his prayer have you prayed personally?

(?) What does Jesus' prayer reveal about his faith and his relationship with God the Father?

(?) How does Satan try to cause Jesus to doubt his purpose? How does Jesus respond to the one who is tempting him?

The Passion of the Christ
(Good Friday and Easter)

Trailer

Accusations, betrayals, and denials

The movie Drama, Rated R

From his anguished prayer in the garden of Gethsemane to his final breath on the cross at Golgotha, this movie portrays what one might have witnessed while following Jesus Christ through the last 12 hours of his life on earth. Between the forces at war to destroy him and the devoted few who love him, Jesus (James Caviezel) takes his final steps down the road he came to walk—a road of suffering and sacrifice for all of mankind.

This clip (about 7 1/2 minutes)

▶ **Start** / 0:23:13 / "Who is this beggar you bring to us?"

■ **Stop** / 0:30:50 / Peter runs from Jesus' gaze.

The religious leaders of the temple send their guards to arrest Jesus and bring him in for questioning. The Pharisees desire to build a case against him so they can put him to death. Various witnesses come forward to levy accusations against Jesus. When Jesus confesses who he is, the Pharisees are horrified, the crowd turns violent, and one of Jesus' followers must decide whether he'll stand with Christ or save himself.

**accusations, lies, denial,
religious leaders, Pharisees,
hypocrisy, fear, self-preservation**

By the Book

Hosea 6:6; Matthew 10:32-33, 26:57-68, 26:69-75, 27:11-25; John 13:36-38

Where to take it

(?) What were the religious leaders trying to prove by asking Jesus what kingdom he came from or reigned over?

(?) Why did the religious leaders of the day find Jesus so threatening?

(?) In this scene, people say various things about Christ. What do they say about him today?

(?) How do religious people warp Jesus' name today?

(?) In what ways can you relate to how Peter behaved?

(?) How do you think Peter felt after the rooster crowed and he realized what he'd done? How would you feel?

(?) Have you ever confessed your unending loyalty to Jesus, only to later deny him in front of friends, family, or even a stranger? Why did the denial happen for you?

131

The Passion of the Christ
(Good Friday and Easter)

Lord, liar, or lunatic?

The movie Drama, Rated R

From his anguished prayer in the garden of Gethsemane to his final breath on the cross at Golgotha, this movie portrays what one might have witnessed while following Jesus Christ through the last 12 hours of his life on earth. Between the forces at war to destroy him and the devoted few who love him, Jesus (James Caviezel) takes his final steps down the road he came to walk—a road of suffering and sacrifice for all of mankind.

This clip (about 4 minutes)

▶ **Start** / 0:38:55 / Jesus is brought before Pontius Pilate.

⏹ **Stop** / 0:42:59 / "What is truth?"

The Pharisees bring Jesus before the regional Roman governor, Pontius Pilate (Hristo Shopov). They want Jesus put to death; but Pilate doesn't believe their charges merit such a punishment. When the Pharisees persist, Pilate has Jesus brought inside to speak with him. Their conversation raises further questions for the governor.

truth, heaven, Jesus' trial, Pharisees, Messiah, guilt, innocence, condemnation

By the Book

Matthew 27:11-25; Mark 10:45; John 4:23-26, 14:6, 18:33-37

Where to take it

? Do you think there are different kinds of truth?

? What is the modern world's answer to Pilate's question: "What is truth?" How would you answer his question?

? When you watch this scene, what does it do to your faith?

? If you were part of the crowd that day, how do you think you would feel about this man they call "the king of the Jews"?

? Why do some people believe Jesus is a liar or a lunatic? What would you say to someone who thinks this way?

? What does it mean when Jesus says, "My kingdom is not of this world"?

? What kind of an impression do you think Jesus left on Pilate's life?

133

Pay It Forward

Trailer

Think of an idea that could
change the world

The movie Drama, Rated PG-13

The ripple effect of performing even the smallest act of kindness can have a
huge impact on others. Eugene Simonet (Kevin Spacey) is a middle school
teacher who offers his seventh grade class an interesting extra-credit project—
think of one idea that can change the world and then put it into action.
Inspired by the opportunity, Trevor McKinney (Haley Joel Osment) comes up
with an original plan that will end up changing his life, his family, and maybe
even the world.

This clip (about 6 minutes)

▶ **Start** / 0:06:15 / Mr. Simonet spins around in his
chair to face his students.

◼ **Stop** / 0:12:22 / Camera focuses in on the
assignment written on the chalkboard.

On the first day of school, the new seventh grade social studies teacher begins
his class by engaging his students in a discussion about their roles in the world.
He wants his students to think beyond where they are at the moment and to
think about what they want for their futures instead. Simonet gives the class a
daring assignment for extra credit: Think of one thing that could change the
world, and then make it happen.

Additional clip (about 3 1/2 minutes)

▶ **Start** / 0:32:58 / "What's paying it forward?"

◼ **Stop** / 0:36:23 / "...I'm going to add variegated, and
I want you to go home tonight..."

Trevor explains to his mom (Helen Hunt) his idea to change the world: "Pay
it forward."

**kindness, serving others, generosity,
faith, action, influence,
change the world around you**

By the Book

Proverbs 3:3, 19:22; Zechariah 7:9-10; Matthew 19:26, 20:30-34; Mark 10:51;
Luke 1:37; Galatians 5:22-23; 1 Timothy 6:18-19; 1 John 5:4

Where to take it

(?) What does *atrophy* mean? Where do you see atrophy in your life?

(?) In Matthew 19:26 and Luke 1:37, Jesus says nothing is impossible for
God. What feels impossible in your life? In your family? In your world?

(?) How would you answer Mr. Simonet's question: *What does the world
expect of you?*

(?) Could the "pay it forward" idea work?

(?) If you were to accept such an assignment, who are the three people
you'd want to help? How would you help them?

(?) What does Scripture say about serving others? About being generous
with your life?

(?) In Matthew 20:32 and Mark 10:51, Jesus asks, "What can I do for you?"
How often do you ask friends, family—even a stranger in need—this
question?

(?) Mr. Simonet tells the class that Trevor's idea requires an extreme act of
faith. What acts of faith have you witnessed in your life?

Pieces of April
(Thanksgiving)

Trailer
Snapshots of family

The movie Comedy/Drama, Rated PG-13

Despite her status as the black sheep of the family, April Burns (Katie Holmes) has invited her estranged relatives to the grungy New York apartment she shares with her boyfriend, Bobby (Derek Luke), for Thanksgiving dinner. While her emotions about the visit seesaw between hope and dread, the oven quits working. Now April must run all over her apartment building to try to find someone who's willing to help her cook the turkey. Meanwhile, her family's journey from the suburbs to New York City isn't much better. They're traveling with a carload of problems, not the least of which is the fact that April's mom, Joy (Patricia Clarkson), is dying of breast cancer and facing her last Thanksgiving. And April's father (Oliver Platt) and siblings (John Gallagher Jr. and Alison Pill) are struggling to cope with it all. So visiting April is a last-ditch effort to make things right, but Joy isn't sure she can deal with another disappointing memory of her daughter.

This clip (about 5 minutes)

▶ **Start** / 1:09:33 / "Don't be hard on yourself, we did the right thing."

■ **Stop** / 1:14:42 / Camera snaps for the last time and the scene fades to black.

April's family stops on the street outside her apartment building but decides not to go inside. Instead they drive to a local restaurant for their Thanksgiving meal. Joy retreats to the bathroom where she unknowingly walks in on an argument between a mother and daughter—a scene that hits too close to home for her. Meanwhile, when April realizes her family came and left without seeing her, she is devastated. But she chooses to make the best of the situation and invites many of the neighbors she met earlier that day to join her for dinner. Then a knock at her door results in a reunion and a memory that April and her mom are certain to cherish for the rest of their lives.

136

By the Book

Psalm 147:3; Ecclesiastes 11:10; Ezekiel 16:44; Malachi 4:6; Matthew 6:14-15

Where to take it

? How do you think you measure up to your parents' expectations?

? What kind of relationship do you have with your parents?

? What kind of relationship did they have with their parents?

? Has your family ever invited other families to share the Thanksgiving meal with you? What was that holiday like?

? When you invite people who may not have a family to come to Thanksgiving, does that diminish the family bond, or does it give new insight to what family and community ought to be or can be?

? April and her mother have been through difficult times together. As you watch the final scene, how does April's mother seem to feel toward her daughter?

? Tell the story of a reconciliation that occurred between you and someone in your family.

Planes, Trains, and Automobiles (Thanksgiving)

Trailer

What does "home" mean to you?

The movie Comedy/Drama, Rated R

Two businessmen trying to get home in time for Thanksgiving are delayed by the effects of a fierce winter storm. Continually thrown together through a series of comic mishaps, Neal Page (Steve Martin) and Del Griffith (John Candy) find themselves struggling to maintain civility as their very different personalities collide. Rigid, uptight Neal is irritated by Del's endless eccentricities, and tension escalates as their initial politeness and patience wear thin and their true feelings about each other surface.

This clip (about 6 minutes)

▶ **Start** / 1:20:46 / "This you?"

■ **Stop** / 1:27:00 / Scene fades to black on Del Griffith's face.

Neal is about to step onto a subway that will take him home just in time for Thanksgiving. Neal has been trying to get home for days, and although he is thankful to be so close, he is even more grateful to be getting rid of his annoying traveling companion. As Neal sits on the subway, he thinks about his wife and children and knows they'll be delighted to see him when he walks through the door. Then Neal remembers a few comments Del made about his own family. Suspecting that Del has been hiding something, Neal goes back to the station to find Del just sitting there, with nowhere to go.

By the Book

Psalm 68:6; Proverbs 22:9; Matthew 25:40; Luke 3:11, 14:12-14;
1 Timothy 6:18; Hebrews 13:2

Where to take it

? Del bluntly tells Neal, "I don't have a home." Do you know anyone who just wanders from place to place with no spot to call home?

? Whom do you think of when you hear the word needy?

? In Luke 14:12-14, whom does the Bible identify as those who need our hospitality?

? Whom do you know of who needs the kind of help you could give?

? What does the Bible say in Hebrews 13:2 about reaching out to others?

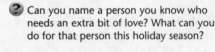

? How could your Thanksgiving be different by giving more than receiving?

? Can you name a person you know who needs an extra bit of love? What can you do for that person this holiday season?

POP CORN

139

Radio

Can we learn something from
everyone?

The movie Drama, Rated PG

In the heart of South Carolina, Coach Harold Jones (Ed Harris) lives a life that revolves around high school football. When he meets a mentally challenged man nicknamed "Radio" (Cuba Gooding Jr.), everything in the coach's life begins to change. Based on a true story, the film chronicles the unlikely friendship that grows between these two men.

This clip (just under 5 minutes)

▶ **Start** / 1:37:38 / "My point is that this man is a disruptive force in our community."

■ **Stop** / 1:42:16 / Coach Jones and his family drive away.

Coach Jones and his family interrupt a town meeting where the people are discussing Radio's future. The coach shares how Radio has impacted his life and unknowingly taught him what is truly important.

140

By the Book

1 Samuel 16:7; Zechariah 7:9-10; Matthew 12:7; Romans 13:10;
Philippians 2:3

Where to take it

- Have you ever known someone with a disability? How did you react to this person?

- What can we learn from people who are different from us?

- How should we treat other people, particularly those who are different from us?

- Coach Jones and Radio developed an unlikely friendship. What qualities do you look for in a friend?

- Is your best friend just like you, or are the two of you very different?

- How did Radio's life influence Coach Jones and his priorities?

- Who has the biggest influence on your life?

- Why is it so difficult to keep our priorities straight? As Christians, what resources do we have to help us determine what is important?

Raising Helen

Trailer

How do we live our lives in a way that will honor those whom we've lost?

The movie Comedy, Rated PG-13

Helen Harris (Kate Hudson) is shocked to learn that after a car accident killed her sister and brother-in-law (Felicity Huffman and Sean O'Bryan), she is now the guardian of their three children: teenager Audrey (Hayden Panettiere), 10-year-old Henry (Spencer Breslin), and kindergartener Sarah (Abigail Breslin). Now Helen must figure out how to balance her new parenting responsibilities with her demanding job at a modeling agency. With the help of a local pastor (John Corbett), Helen and the kids learn how to become a family.

This clip (just under 3 minutes)

▶ **Start** / 1:24:47 / Henry's team is practicing basketball drills.

■ **Stop** / 1:27:22 / Henry takes a shot.

Henry loves playing basketball, yet he refuses to participate with his new team. Helen shows up at the end of a practice hoping to figure out why Henry doesn't want to play. When she discovers he's afraid he'll be dishonoring his father's memory by playing without Dad, Helen reassures Henry that he can honor his father by continuing to live his life and by cherishing the memories they shared.

By the Book

Psalm 34:18, 56:8; John 16:20; 1 Thessalonians 4:13; Revelation 21:4

Where to take it

? Have you ever lost a loved one? What emotions did you experience?

? Did you ever feel guilty about laughing or smiling? Why?

? Why is it important for us to continue living our lives after we lose someone?

? Where can we find comfort when we are grieving?

? How can we make time to remember someone we've lost?

? How can we encourage someone who has lost a loved one?

? Compare and contrast your responses to the death of someone who *didn't* have a relationship with God with that of the death of someone who lived life for God's glory.

? How do you hope people will remember you after you're gone? What kind of legacy do you hope to leave?

The Santa Clause (Christmas)

Do you deny how God made you?

The movie Comedy, Rated PG

Divorced father Scott Calvin (Tim Allen) is a busy toy executive who seems to have everything at his fingertips—except time to spend with his son Charlie (Eric Lloyd). On Christmas Eve, Charlie is convinced he hears Santa on the roof. When Scott goes outside to investigate, he startles the stranger in a red suit who slips and falls off the roof. Unable to awaken their visitor, Charlie convinces his dad to try on Santa's coat, which, unbeknownst to Scott, makes him the new Santa. Scott begins to experience many changes over the next year as he gains weight, grows a white beard, and somehow knows who is naughty and who is nice. While Scott's colleagues and ex-wife think he's lost his sanity, Charlie knows everything is as it should be so his father can take on the role of Santa Claus.

This clip (about 5 1/2 minutes)

▶ **Start** / 0:57:53 / Scott is running on a treadmill.

◼ **Stop** / 1:03:33 / "What am I supposed to do with all these packages? Come on ! Ah!"

Scott Calvin's body is changing; he grows a full beard in a matter of hours and the digital numbers on his bathroom scale keep climbing higher and higher while he's still standing on it. Not only is his doctor (Steve Vinovich) at a loss to explain his symptoms, but his ex-wife, Laura (Wendy Crewson), and her husband, Neal (Judge Reinhold), are also shocked by the dramatic changes in his appearance. As the evidence keeps piling up, Scott begins to realize there is no escaping the fact: he is indeed transforming into Santa Claus.

144

By the Book

Luke 12:48b; Romans 12:2; Philippians 3:20-21; 2 Timothy 1:7; James 1:17

Where to take it

? What do you enjoy doing?

? If you could do anything at all with your life, what would you choose to do?

? What gifts do you think God gave you to use on this earth?

? Have you ever run away from your talents because you didn't know if you wanted to accept them?

? Because of his new identity, Scott's body starts changing before his mind and his attitude catch up. What does the Bible say in Romans 12:2 about transformation?

? What parts of us change when we first trust Christ? What parts of us change as we continue to trust in Christ?

? Compare and contrast the growth process of a Christian to what the character in this movie experiences.

Saved!

Trailer

All in the name of God

The movie Comedy, Rated PG-13

Just before her senior year at a Christian high school begins, Mary (Jena Malone) becomes pregnant. As the school year progresses, Mary has to deal with the consequences of her choices. When her secret is discovered, she is suddenly alienated and alone. Mary begins to question not only her faith in God, but also those who claim to follow him.

This clip (about 2 minutes)

▶ **Start** / 0:39:12 / "After we win the costume contest..."

◼ **Stop** / 0:41:08 / Mary runs down the sidewalk.

The high school principal and pastor (Martin Donovan) assigns a rescue mission to Hilary Faye (Mandy Moore), Mary's former friend and the school's paragon of Christian zealotry—comfort Mary and guide her back to her faith.

By the Book

Leviticus 19:15; Luke 6:37, 12:1-3; Romans 2:1; Galatians 6:1; Colossians 3:12-14

Where to take it

(?) What is your response to this scene—is it unreal or eerily true? Do you know Christians who behave this way?

(?) Have you ever faced condemnation and judgment from someone who proclaimed to be a Christian? How did that incident change your opinion of that person?

(?) What does the word *hypocrisy* mean to you? Do you know any hypocrites? Do you believe all Christians are hypocrites to some degree?

(?) Would Hilary Faye be considered a modern-day Pharisee? What does Jesus say in Luke 12:1-3 about Pharisees?

(?) How do we get God's Word wrong?

(?) As she throws her Bible at Mary, Hilary Faye exclaims, "I am *filled* with Jesus' love!" Why do some Christians feel the need to tell people how holy they are?

(?) Mary tells Hilary Faye that the Bible is not a weapon. What are some of the ways the world uses the Bible to hurt others?

(?) How do you think Jesus feels about Christians who hurt other people—emotionally or even physically—in his name?

Trailer

Is one man's life worth
another man's death?

The movie   Action/Drama, Rated R

In the midst of World War II, the government receives word of a family in Iowa
who has tragically lost three of their four sons on the battlefield. A squad of D-
Day survivors, under the command of Captain John Miller (Tom Hanks), is sent
behind enemy lines to rescue the remaining son, Private Ryan (Matt Damon),
and bring him home.

This clip   (6 minutes)

▶ **Start** / 2:36:00 / "They're tank busters, sir,
P-51's."

◼ **Stop** / 2:42:00 / An American flag waves in the
wind.

Private Ryan is devastated when he receives word that his brothers have died;
however, he refuses to abandon his army brothers. Seeing the depth of Ryan's
commitment, Captain Miller and his men join the outnumbered company to
defend a village against the Germans. After a deadly German tank assault,
Miller maneuvers his remaining men to the bridge at the edge of town. When
Miller is fatally wounded in the process, Ryan kneels beside him as Capt. Miller
issues a final order. Years later, as Ryan stands before a tombstone at Arlington
National Cemetery, he remembers Captain Miller and wonders if his life has
been worthy of such a sacrifice.

By the Book

Jeremiah 1:19; Lamentations 3:32; John 15:13; 2 Corinthians 5:14-15;
Galatians 5:14; 2 Timothy 2:1-4; 1 John 3:16

Where to take it

- Do you think freedom is worth fighting for? Why or why not?

- When you think about all the American soldiers who've sacrificed their lives for freedom, how do you feel? Is there anything for which you'd give your life?

- Do you think Americans truly appreciate all the freedoms we enjoy? To what extent do you take your freedom for granted?

- Do you think people have become numb to the sacrifices of soldiers? To the sacrifice of Christ?

- What sacrifices are Christians called to make as soldiers of Christ?

- Do you think one man's life is worth the loss of another? Why or why not?

- What parallels do you see between the lives of Capt. Miller and Jesus?

- What do you think about Capt. Miller's last words to Private Ryan? How are they different from what Christ says to us about the sacrifice he made for you?

149

Say Anything (Graduation)

 Trailer

What happens after high school?

The movie Drama/Romance, Rated PG-13

Lloyd Dobler (John Cusack) is a charming and likable guy who has little ambition or direction for his future. Diane Court (Ione Skye) has been an overachiever her whole life, but she is mostly alienated from her peers by her father (John Mahoney), who has his own plans for her success. Lloyd is infatuated with valedictorian Diane, who wouldn't be able to pick Lloyd out of a crowd. But Lloyd dares to dream big, and after he asks Diane on a date, the two discover a genuine affection for each other. However, Diane's father is concerned that her relationship with Lloyd will cloud her judgment about her future. Diane has plans to leave for college in England at the end of the summer, and now she must decide whether or not Lloyd can be a part of that picture.

This clip (about 2 minutes)

▶ **Start** / 0:03:57 / "Thank you."

■ **Stop** / 0:06:15 / "I...am...really...scared."

At the Lakewood High School graduation, the principal (Charles Walker) introduces Diane before she makes her valedictorian speech entitled "Soaring Ahead." As she looks upon her disinterested classmates, most of whom she doesn't even know, Diane speaks to her peers about her hopes and fears for the future.

By the Book

Psalm 94:19; Proverbs 16:3; Jeremiah 29:11-13; Matthew 6:25-34;
John 14:27

Where to take it

2. Where do you see yourself five years from now? In 10 years?

2. Do you think you will have positive or negative memories of your time in high school? Why?

2. What are your dreams for your future?

2. In what ways do your parents support or discourage you in pursuing those dreams?

2. What would you do differently from your parents in regard to life dreams?

2. What worries do you have when you think about life after high school? Read Matthew 6:25-34. What does the Bible have to say about worry?

2. What's it going to take for you to find success and happiness in your future?

School of Rock

Trailer

Are you using your gifts and talents?

The movie   Comedy, Rated PG-13

When slacker Dewey Finn (Jack Black) finds himself fired from the rock band he started, he realizes he may have to give up the one thing in life that inspires him the most—music. In a desperate attempt to appease his frustrated roommate (Mike White) and find a way to pay the rent, Dewey takes a substitute-teaching job at a stuffy private school. At first his laid-back attitude clashes with the strict rules and regulations his students are used to. But then he listens in on a music lesson and uncovers a classroom full of musical talent. Dewey's dream of competing in the Battle of the Bands is brought back to life as he helps his students find and utilize the talents they have in a totally new way.

This clip   (about 7 minutes)

▶ **Start** / 0:20:33 / Students enter the classroom.

⏹ **Stop** / 0:27:45 / "When we get back from lunch, I'll assign the rest of you *killer* positions!"

After realizing that his students are already able to play many different instruments, Dewey begins to plan how he can shape his class into a rock band. He brings his own instruments into the classroom and allows the students to demonstrate their skills—but with his rock music influence. As he begins to connect with his students on a whole new level, Dewey explains to them that each individual has a place, a purpose, and a spot that only he or she can fill.

gifts, talents, abilities, experience,
heaven, legacy, worth, dreams,
serving others

By the Book

Matthew 6:26, 25:21; Romans 12:4-5; 1 Corinthians 1:27-31, 12:4;
Ephesians 4:7-13; Philippians 2:12-13; James 1:17

Where to take it

(?) Name at least one gift you feel you possess. What things do others say
you do well?

(?) How could your gifts and abilities be used to bless others?

(?) In this clip, many people come together and use their unique talents
for one purpose. In 1 Corinthians 1:27-31, how does the body of Christ
work the same way?

(?) Read Matthew 25:21. What does "Well done, good and faithful servant"
mean?

(?) Philippians 2:12-13 tells us to "work out" our salvation.
What does this mean to you?

(?) If fear of failure weren't an issue, what would you
want to do with your life?

(?) Twenty years from now when you look
back on your life, what regrets do you
hope to avoid?

(?) What action steps are you
taking to achieve your
goals and dreams? What
role does God play in
those dreams?

Scrooged
(Christmas)

Trailer

Does your life need a change?

The movie Fantasy/Comedy, Rated PG-13

Frank Cross (Bill Murray) is a television network president who— at the expense of his family and coworkers—is consumed only with himself and his career. However, Frank is just following in the footsteps of his former boss, Lew Hayward (John Forsythe), who's been dead for a few years now. But on Christmas Eve, Lew pays Frank a visit from beyond the grave and warns him that three mysterious strangers will be stopping by to see him throughout the night. As Frank takes a strange trip through his life, his loves, and his choices, he discovers a new perspective on Christmas.

This clip (about 4 1/2 minutes)

▶ **Start** / 0:18:06 / Frank Cross pours a drink in his office.

■ **Stop** / 0:22:32 / Lew says, "You can be saved. You've got time."

After accepting an undeserved humanitarian award, Frank returns to his office where he trashes the trophy and heads for the whiskey. When the door to his office blows off its hinges, Frank sees his former boss, Lew, standing there. Lew has come back from the dead to caution Frank about his life and urge him to turn from his ways before it's too late. Being a modern-day Scrooge, Frank simply dismisses the visit and the advice.

154

By the Book

Proverbs 18:12; Luke 12:33; Philippians 2:3; Colossians 3:12-14, 17; Hebrews 13:2

Where to take it

? The ghost tells Frank, "Don't waste your life." How can a person waste his or her life?

? If someone from your past told you to change the way you live your life, would you heed the warning, or would you think it was crazy?

? What is an area of your life that needs to change?

? "Mankind should have been my business. Don't wait to get yourself involved." What does this quote from the scene prompt you to think or feel?

? Can you look back on your life and see some regrets already beginning to form? Does it make you want to change your future?

? What are some of your non-negotiable values that you want your life to stand for?

? Describe how important it is—to you personally—that those around you are taken care of.

? What would you say is the most important thing in your life?

Seabiscuit

Trailer

Everybody is good for something

The movie Drama, Rated PG-13

In the late 1930s, America was paralyzed by the Great Depression. A disheartened businessman, Charles Howard (Jeff Bridges); a washed-up horse trainer, Tom Smith (Chris Cooper); and a half-blind jockey, Red Pollard (Tobey Maguire) are brought together by an undersized racehorse who ultimately gave new hope to three downtrodden men and lifted the spirits of an entire nation.

This clip (just over 2 1/2 minutes)

▶ **Start** / 0:39:44 / "I don't know, maybe you want a smaller barn. Somebody who can take the time to..."

■ **Stop** / 0:42:27 / Charles takes a sip of the coffee Tom has just poured.

Charles spots Tom when he is out looking for a potential racehorse and barn. More in tune with animals than with people, Tom spends his time with broken-down horses rather than in winner's circles. Charles is intrigued by Tom and goes out to talk to him at his campfire.

By the Book

Leviticus 19:15; Deuteronomy 15:7; Psalm 72:13, 103:2-5; Proverbs 27:19; Ecclesiastes 9:11; Jeremiah 29:11-13; Luke 9:48; Romans 5:8

Where to take it

- Why is it important to take the time to love the unlovable? Whom do you consider to be unlovable?

- Scripture has a lot to say in verses like Leviticus 19:15, Deuteronomy 15:7, and Luke 9:48 about "the least" or the needy. After you read some of the passages, in what ways do you live this out?

- What are some simple ways you can leave your comfort zone to see the good in people?

- Tom tells Charles, "You know, you don't throw a whole life away just because it's banged up a little." What does that mean to you when you think about your friends? Your family? Yourself? Others?

- Tom could see that each horse was good for a purpose. How has someone believed in you when you might not have deserved it?

- What does it mean to "treat people like you want them to become"?

- How does believing in others make a difference in the way they see themselves? How does it change the way they behave?

Trailer

Is beauty only skin deep?

The movie Animation/Comedy, Rated PG

Just back from their honeymoon, Shrek (voiced by Mike Myers) and Princess Fiona (voiced by Cameron Diaz) are invited to visit Fiona's parents (voiced by John Cleese and Julie Andrews) in the kingdom of Far, Far Away. Though everyone is excited about meeting Fiona's new husband, no one expects to see two ogres step out of the royal carriage. It doesn't take long for Shrek to realize he is far from the match Fiona's parents would have made for their only daughter. And when Fairy Godmother (voiced by Jennifer Saunders) discovers that her son, Prince Charming (voiced by Rupert Everett), has missed his chance to marry Fiona, she vows to write a new "happily ever after" that does *not* include Shrek.

This clip (about 5 minutes)

- ▶ **Start** / 1:15:25 / Shrek says, "Stop!" and rides down the castle stairs.

- ■ **Stop** / 1:20:39 / Shrek and Fiona kiss.

Thinking it will make Fiona happy, Shrek drinks a potion that turns him into a handsome man. When Fairy Godmother sees his transformation, she has him captured. Then she convinces Fiona's father to put a potion in his daughter's tea that will cause Fiona to fall in love with Prince Charming when he kisses her. Shrek escapes and races to the castle to see if he can save Fiona from Charming and his meddling mother.

By the Book

1 Samuel 16:7; Proverbs 31:30; John 7:24; Galatians 5:14; Philippians 2:3

Where to take it

(?) What do you look for in a boyfriend or girlfriend?

(?) What do you think your future spouse will look like?

(?) How important is physical beauty to you?

(?) What attracts you to someone?

(?) When other people look at you, what do you think they see? Do you think you are appealing as a boyfriend, girlfriend, or spouse?

(?) Shrek offers to completely change his appearance if it would make Fiona happy. Would you make such a sacrifice for someone you loved?

(?) Do you think your identity as a person is linked to your appearance? How so?

(?) Would you have made the same choice Princess Fiona made? Explain.

Spider-Man 2

Trailer

How far would you go to save
someone?

The movie Drama, Rated PG-13

To everyone around him, Peter Parker (Tobey Maguire) is a mild-mannered
physics student at Columbia University. When there's trouble in the city,
however, he becomes the web-slinging superhero—Spider-Man. Unfortunately
nothing seems to be going right for Peter as he tries to juggle his double life.
Serving the greater good has already cost him his job, and he nearly flunked
out of school. When some of his super powers begin to fail and his friendships
become strained, Peter must decide if his destiny is to live a normal life or to
continue protecting the city as Spider-Man.

This clip (just over 4 1/2 minutes)

▶ **Start** / 1:37:00 / Doc Ock's arm crashes through
the train window.

■ **Stop** / 1:41:35 / "It's good to have you back,
Spider-Man."

When a fusion experiment goes horribly wrong, a new villain is born. Brilliant
physicist Dr. Otto Octavius (Alfred Molina) is transformed into Doc Ock: half-
man, half-machine with four powerful tentacles fused into his spine. When Doc
Ock takes Mary Jane (Kirsten Dunst) captive, Peter resumes the role of Spider-
Man in order to save her. During a face-off with Doc Ock, Spider-Man must
find a way to stop a speeding train full of passengers headed for disaster.

By the Book

2 Chronicles 15:7; Psalm 31:24; Matthew 16:24-26; Mark 10:45; John 15:13; Ephesians 6:12; 1 Timothy 4:12

Where to take it

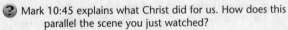

? How do you think you might react in a moment of danger or crisis—would your first instinct be to save your own life or to help others?

? Mark 10:45 explains what Christ did for us. How does this parallel the scene you just watched?

? How far would you go to save another person?

? In John 15:13, Jesus says that there is no greater love than a friend giving his life for a friend. What about giving your life for a complete stranger?

? Name three things you want your life to be about.

? How do you share God's love with your friends—or with complete strangers? How do your actions "share" your faith?

? As Christians, what is our responsibility when it comes to fighting evil in the world?

The Stepford Wives

Trailer

What is a woman's place in society?

The movie — Comedy/Drama, Rated PG-13

High-powered television executive Joanna Eberhart (Nicole Kidman) is fired from her job after a reality show she created takes a tragic turn. Joanna's husband, Walter (Matthew Broderick), decides to move their family to the charming town of Stepford, Connecticut, an exclusive community filled with beautiful homes, wealthy families—and a secret that could tear Joanna and Walter apart.

This clip (about 7 minutes)

▶ **Start** / 1:03:29 / "Ever since we met, you've beaten me at everything."

■ **Stop** / 1:10:44 / Scene goes to a bright white.

When Joanna figures out what is going on in Stepford, she confronts the men at their social club, where women are forbidden and where the leader of the town, Mike Wellington (Christopher Walken), calls all the shots. What she discovers about Mike's plans and her husband's insecurities may mean the end for her.

**obedience, dominance, love,
equally yoked, power,
men versus women**

By the Book

Proverbs 31:10-31; Hosea 6:6; Malachi 2:14-15; Ephesians 5:22, 5:25;
1 Peter 3:1, 3:7

Where to take it

(?) What is a man's role in a relationship? In a marriage? In society?

(?) Do you think women should have a certain role in society?

(?) Read Proverbs 31:10-31. What does the Bible say about a woman's role? Does this hold true in the modern world?

(?) Could our culture ever get to the point of a Stepford-like cloning of a certain type of woman? Do we do this in any way within our own culture? If so, how?

(?) Do you think our culture advocates and celebrates a healthy concept of what a woman should be? Do you agree or disagree with society's image of women?

(?) Describe the traits of a "Stepford Christian." In what ways do you feel the pressure to be a certain way when it comes to your church community?

(?) Joanna asks her husband if he would rather have robotic devotion or real love. If you were to ask God that question, what do you think his response would be? Why?

(?) Read Hosea 6:6. What is this verse saying about what God desires from you?

The Sure Thing

Trailer

What would you do for a sure thing?

The movie Comedy/Romance, Rated PG-13

Walter "Gib" Gibson (John Cusack) is a freshman in his first semester at a small
northeastern college where he's found both the weather and the women to be
bitter cold. His fortunes seem to be improving when his old high school buddy
(Anthony Edwards) calls from sunny Southern California with an offer Gib can't
refuse: the chance to sleep with a girl (Nicolette Sheridan) with no questions
asked and no strings attached—a "sure thing." With no money for an airline
ticket but with an urgent need to get to California, he manages to find a ride
posted on a bulletin board at school. He soon discovers he'll be sharing the trip
with a girl from his English class, Alison Bradbury (Daphne Zuniga), who is also
traveling to Los Angeles to see her fiancé (Boyd Gaines). When the travelers
run into trouble, Gib and Alison, who couldn't be more different, are strangely
drawn to one another. When they finally arrive in California, Gib must decide
which he would rather have: a real relationship or a sure thing.

This clip (about 3 1/2 minutes)

▶ **Start** / 1:27:41 / Scene opens with an outdoor
shot of students going to class.

■ **Stop** / 1:31:21 / "She wasn't my type."

Gib and Alison have returned to campus after Christmas break. The last time
they saw each other, Alison walked away from Gib to be with her fiancé, and
Gib resolved to forget Alison in the arms of his sure thing. Now back in English
class, Professor Taub (Viveca Lindfors) reads Gib's essay about his experience.

By the Book

Psalm 37:4; Proverbs 27:19; Ecclesiastes 11:9; Romans 13:13;
1 Corinthians 6:16-20; 1 Thessalonians 4:3

Where to take it

(?) What do you think of the choice Gib made?

(?) Gib's essay describes the kind of girl he always dreamed of being with. What do you think about the traits he lists?

(?) What qualities do you look for in a person you'd like to date?

(?) The concept of the sure thing (as defined earlier in the movie) is being able to have sex with someone with no questions asked, no strings attached, and no guilt involved. Do you think this is possible? Explain.

(?) Read 1 Corinthians 6:16-20. What does the Bible say about sex?

(?) What is the difference between sex and intimacy?

(?) Do you think sex can be separated from love—in other words, is it possible to have one without the other? Explain.

(?) Gib couldn't tell his sure thing what she wanted to hear; he realized for the first time that the words "I love you" were no longer just words to him. What do you think he meant by that?

The Terminal

The movie Drama, Rated PG-13

In the time it took to fly across the Atlantic Ocean, Viktor Navorski (Tom Hanks) has become a man without a country. A coup in his homeland causes a diplomatic dilemma that leaves Viktor stuck in the international lounge of the John F. Kennedy Airport with no valid passport, no friends, no U.S. currency, and no ability to speak the language. While Viktor quickly learns about American culture and how to make it work for him, the airport authorities try to figure out what to do with Viktor Navorski.

This clip (about 2 1/2 minutes)

▶ **Start** / 1:37:55 / "You're living at Gate 67. I just want to know why."

⏹ **Stop** / 1:40:41 / "Maybe I think he do it for me."

Viktor teaches himself English and befriends some airport employees and other people who regularly pass through the terminal. One of Viktor's new acquaintances is flight attendant Amelia Warren (Catherine Zeta-Jones). Amelia assumes Viktor is a man who travels a lot for his work, until she discovers he's been living in the terminal for nine months. Viktor tells her why he has traveled such a great distance to New York City and endured the long stay in the airport.

By the Book

Genesis 17:7; Numbers 30:2; Deuteronomy 4:31, 7:9; Job 5:11; Proverbs 22:1; Isaiah 43:1; Matthew 5:33-37

Where to take it

? How important is a promise to you?

? How serious are you about keeping your promises?

? Describe a time when you made a promise to someone. How did you follow through?

? Viktor goes to great lengths to keep his promise to his father, knowing his father would have done the same for him. What promises from our heavenly Father are the most meaningful to you?

? Describe a time when you personally experienced one of God's promises.

? What promises to God do you need to keep?

? In this scene, many famous names are pulled out of an old peanut jar. Read Proverbs 22:1. What do you think that verse is saying?

? Isaiah 43:1 says, "I have summoned you by name; you are mine." What does this mean to you?

The Village

Trailer

Are the sins from your
past chasing you?

The movie Drama, Rated PG-13

The residents of Covington, Pennsylvania enjoy a peaceful, simple, old-
fashioned existence—marred only by their fear of mysterious creatures lurking
in the woods around the village. Though an ancient treaty exists between the
villagers and the creatures, signs indicate that the treaty has been broken and
the people of Covington are in danger. When upstart Lucius Hunt (Joaquin
Phoenix) begins to question the elders' wisdom in isolating the village from
medical aid, Covington's simple yet strict way of life is shaken, and the years
of peace in the village are over.

This clip (7 minutes—very few words are
used in the scene)

▶ **Start** / 1:19:00 / Ivy falls into a deep pit.

⏹ **Stop** / 1:26:00 / The creature falls into the pit.

When her beloved Lucius is badly wounded, Ivy Walker (Bryce Dallas Howard)
offers to journey into the dangerous woods to "the towns" and bring back
the medicine that will save him—despite the handicap of her blindness and
her fear of the unknown creatures. After her companions panic and leave
her behind in the forest, Ivy forces herself to continue her quest through the
darkness and then stumbles into a deep pit. But her determination overcomes
her fear, and Ivy frees herself in time to use the very pit that trapped her to
her advantage.

**freedom in Christ, sin, the past,
courage, condemnation, faith,
oppression, fear**

By the Book

Psalm 103:12; Proverbs 5:22; Isaiah 43:18; Romans 8:1, 8:35-39;
Philippians 3:12-14; 1 Timothy 5:24-25; Hebrews 11:1; 1 John 1:9

Where to take it

? Have you ever felt stranded or trapped in a situation as Ivy finds herself
trapped in the pit?

? Did you feel Ivy's fear as the monster
relentlessly chases her through the trees?
In what ways do you feel as though your
past is stalking you? What about a sin or
a secret?

? What does the Bible have to say in
Proverbs 5:22 about sin chasing and
finding us? How does this help you to
understand sin and the power it has?

? Why do we spend so much time trying
to hide or cover up our secret sins, when
in reality they're as visible as the monster
in this scene?

? Ivy is able to defeat the creature only
when she turns to face it head-on. What parts of your life need to be
faced with courage and then dropped into a pit to be left behind and
forgotten?

? Read Psalm 103:12. What does God say he will do with our sin in order
to renew us?

? Romans 8:1 tells us there will be no condemnation for those who are in
Christ Jesus. What does this mean to you?

? Ivy doesn't allow her blindness to prevent her from conquering the
creature. How does the blind faith, described in Hebrews 11:1, help us to
conquer our demons?

Win a Date with Tad Hamilton!

(Valentine's Day—for the guys)

Trailer

What does love look like?

The movie Comedy/Romance, Rated PG-13

Beautiful, small-town Rosalee Futch (Kate Bosworth) enters a contest to win a dream date with her favorite actor and Hollywood hunk—Tad Hamilton (Josh Duhamel). Rosie wins the contest and is flown to California for the date. While she enjoys her time with Tad, she doesn't allow herself to be swept away by him. Tad, on the other hand, comes away from the evening smitten with Rosalee. Dissatisfied with all that's lacking in his Tinseltown existence, Tad decides to fly to Rosie's hometown so he can spend more time with her. Everyone seems crazy about the idea, except Rosie's closest friend, Pete (Topher Grace), who realizes that if he doesn't do something soon, he may lose the girl he loves.

This clip (about 4 minutes)

▶ **Start** / 0:59:21 / "I finally did it! People, are you watching this? Rosie!"

◼ **Stop** / 1:03:07 / "No—my bad. Finish up in here. I'm sorry."

Pete has spent all his energy trying to get Rosie to forget about Tad Hamilton. When it becomes obvious that Tad has won Rosie's affection, Pete corners and confronts Tad regarding his intentions toward Rosie. With no way to escape, Tad must listen as Pete shares what he cherishes most about Rosie and what he'll do to Tad if he breaks her heart.

By the Book

Song of Songs 7:10, 8:6; Matthew 19:4-6; John 13:34-35; Philippians 2:1-4

Where to take it

(?) Have you ever lost someone close to you because that person was taken away and there was nothing you could do but let that person go? Describe your story.

(?) Describe some of the best traits of someone you care about.

(?) If someone were to fall in love with you, what would you want that person to know about you?

(?) Pete describes Rosie's six different smiles. Is there anyone in your life who knows you that well?

(?) What does the Song of Songs say about adoring your mate?

(?) How do you think you'll know when you've found the person you're meant to marry?

(?) When you think about the future, do you see yourself spending the rest of your life with one person? Why or why not?

Win a Date with Tad Hamilton!
(Valentine's Day—for the girls)

Trailer

What does love look like?

The movie   Comedy/Romance, Rated PG-13

Beautiful, small-town Rosalee Futch (Kate Bosworth) enters a contest to win a dream date with her favorite actor and Hollywood hunk—Tad Hamilton (Josh Duhamel). Rosie wins the contest and is flown to California for the date. While she enjoys her time with Tad, she doesn't allow herself to be swept away by him. Tad, on the other hand, comes away from the evening smitten with Rosalee. Dissatisfied with all that's lacking in his Tinseltown existence, Tad decides to fly to Rosie's hometown so he can spend more time with her. Everyone seems crazy about the idea, except Rosie's closest friend, Pete (Topher Grace), who realizes that if he doesn't do something soon, he may lose his great love.

This clip   (about 6 minutes)

▶ **Start** / 1:25:10 / Rosalee gets out of a taxi in the pouring rain.

■ **Stop** / 1:31:20 / Pete and Rosie dance as THE END appears on the screen.

Tad lands a big movie role and asks Rosie to go with him on location. The night before they leave, Pete makes a last-ditch attempt to let Rosie know he loves her. Although confused by Pete's ill-timed profession, Rosie tells him she can't change her plans. While on their way to California, Tad confesses he wasn't honest with Rosie when he talked her into going with him. When Tad shares what Pete said about her six different smiles, Rosie realizes it's time to go back home.

172

By the Book

Genesis 2:24; Leviticus 21:13; Psalm 34:18; Song of Songs 7:10;
Hosea 2:19-20; 1 Corinthians 7:2, 7:9, 11:3; 2 Corinthians 6:14;
Ephesians 5:23, 33; 1 Timothy 1:5; Hebrews 13:4

Where to take it

- Angelica (Kathryn Hahn) tells Rosie that when great love is rejected, something inside dies. Have you ever experienced rejection? How did it affect you?

- Describe a time when everything around you reminded you of a lost love.

- Do you fear you may miss out on the great love of your life? What circumstances have brought about that fear?

- What do you look for in a dating partner? What do you look for in a spouse? Are they the same qualities or characteristics?

- Read Leviticus 21:13, 1 Corinthians 7:2, 2 Corinthians 6:14, and Ephesians 5:23, 33. What does the Bible say about how to find and treat your mate?

- What does the Bible say in Genesis 2:24 about where your spouse should be on your priority list?

- Have you experienced a divorce in your family? How does that affect your plans for your own marriage?

Trailer

Why am I here?

The movie Comedy, Rated PG-13

Derek Zoolander (Ben Stiller) is a self-obsessed mega model and so empty-headed that he doesn't realize that his various trademark looks are the same tight-lipped pose. Derek is confident he is still at the top of his game even though hot new model Hansel (Owen Wilson) has arrived on the scene. Through a series of misfortunes, Derek begins to question his place in the world of fashion. He decides to retire but is soon lured back into modeling when he is offered a deal to present a new line for world-renowned designer Mugatu (Will Ferrell). What Derek doesn't realize is that Mugatu has darker ideas for how he wants to use Derek, which have little to do with his skills as a model.

This clip (about 3 minutes)

▶ **Start** / 0:11:28 / Derek comes out of the backstage door.

■ **Stop** / 0:14:44 / "Come on, man. Come on!"

Having been crowned VH1's Male Model of the Year for three years straight, Derek is again vying for the top prize in the male modeling world. Derek's main competition is newcomer Hansel, who has been nominated in his first year of modeling. When Hansel is announced to be the winner, Derek struts up to the platform oblivious to the fact that his name wasn't called. He begins his acceptance speech in front of a stunned crowd, while the real winner, Hansel, steps onstage to accept the award. This embarrassing turn of events causes Derek to question who he is and what he is doing with his life. Though Derek's roommates—Brint, Rufus, and Meekus (Alexandre Manning, Asio Highsmith, and Alexander Skarsgård)—try to help him through his dark hour, Derek begins to realize that his questions about his life's purpose may be a little too deep for his image-driven friends.

By the Book

1 Samuel 16:7b; Proverbs 3:5-6, 16:9; Jeremiah 29:11-13; Romans 8:28

Where to take it

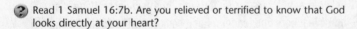

(?) Have you ever asked the question, "What am I on this earth for?" What answers did you find?

(?) What are some things that can cause us to question our true purposes? What can we do to overcome or combat those questions?

(?) What do you think God wants you to do with your life?

(?) Like Derek, name a time when a humiliating experience became a turning point for you.

(?) Someone once said, "Pain is a terrific teacher." What do you think is true about this statement?

(?) Do you see yourself through the world's eyes or through God's eyes? How do you see other people?

(?) Read 1 Samuel 16:7b. Are you relieved or terrified to know that God looks directly at your heart?